WIREMAN SECOND YEAR MCQ

OBJECTIVE QUESTION ANSWERS

MANOJ DOLE

Digitization is the need of the time. In the future, training in industrial training institutes will need to be conducted using online internet to make training more convenient and easy. E-books containing a set of MCQ questions will be made available to the trainees as they need to be more accustomed to the multiple choice questions MCQ to prepare for the online exams taking place in their industrial training institutes.

With all these factors in mind, Mr. Manoj Madhukar Dole Instructor, Industrial Training Institute, Satara, has written books according to the new annual system and NSQF-5 syllabus. And they've created theoretical mobile apps and blogs to make training easier, and made all these educational materials available for download on the world famous websites Google Play Store, Amazon and Apple Book Store.

The books were published by Hon'ble Joint Director Shri Rajendra Ghume Saheb Regional Office of Vocational Education and Training, Pune on 9/1/2019, at this time Shri Prakash Saigavkar Saheb Principal Government Industrial Training Institute Aundh Pune, Shri Tukaram Misal Saheb Principal Govt. Q. Sanstha Satara, Shri Sachin Dhumal Saheb District Vocational Education and Training Officer Satara, Shri Yatin Pargaonkar Saheb Principal Govt. Q. Sanstha Kolhapur, Shri Vikas Teke Saheb Inspector Vocational Education and Training Regional Office Pune, Palekar Foods Products Pvt. Ltd. Entrepreneurial Chairman of Satara Mr. Nilkanthrao Palekar Saheb, Chairman of Hira Foods Mr. Ibrahim Baba Tamboli Saheb, Mrs. Shalmali Pawar Headmaster Government Technical School Center Satara and other dignitaries were present on the occasion.

Contents

Prologue

Wireman Second Year MCQ is a simple Book for ITI Engineering Course Wireman Second Year, NSQF-4 Syllabus in 2022, It contains objective questions with underlined & bold correct answers MCQ covering all topics including all about to construct and test Half–wave, full-wave, and bridge rectifiers with filter & without filter. He will be able to identify the constructional features, working principles of DC machine. Starting with suitable starter, running, forward and reverse operation and speed control of DC motors. Conduct the load performance test of DC machine with due care and safety. Maintain and troubleshoot of DC machines. He will recognise the constructional features, working principles of single phase and 3 phase AC motors. Starting with suitable starter, running, forward and reverse operation and speed control of AC motors with due care and safety. He should be able to identify the constructional features, working principles of Alternator set. Test, Wire-up and run alternator. Synchronization of Alternator with due care and safety, identify the types, constructional features, working principles of transformer (single & three phase) Connect and test Transformer. He should be able to prepare single line diagram and layout plan of electrical transmission & distribution systems and power plants with knowledge of principle applied. Make and test power connection to substation equipments with care and safety. He will select, assemble, test and wire-up control panel, plan, estimate and costing of different types of wiring system as per Indian Electricity rule, and lots more.

We add new question answers with each new version. Please email us in case of any errors/omissions. This is arguably the largest and best Book for All engineering multiple choice questions and answers.

As a student you can use it for your exam prep. This e-Book is also useful for professors to refresh material.

Foreword

Vocational education and training is imparted through the Department of Vocational Education and Training through the Department of Business Education and Business Practical to supply multi-skilled artisans in line with the rapidly growing demand in the industrial sector in the 21st century. All the occupations within the institutions are important, as the trainees from these occupations develop multi-skills as per the demands of the industry.

with the noble intention of making available MCQ e-books suitable for all businesses, considering that all the examinations in all the industries in the industrial sector are conducted online and include MCQ method questions. Mr. Manoj Madhukar Dole has written a very good e-book on MCQ method as per the new annual syllabus. This e-book will definitely be a guide for all the trainees, trainee candidates, training instructors and others concerned.

The author of the book is Mr. Manoj Madhukar Dole, Instructor Gov. ITI Satara has 17 years of training experience. Written as a new annual pattern, this e-book incorporates modern digital QR Code technology to understand the layout, simple language, and simple syntax, diagrams and videos for each subject. So I am sure that this e-book will definitely be useful for in-depth study and exam practice. The work they have done is certainly commendable.

Mr. Tukaram Misal
Principal Government Industrial Training Institute Satara.

Preface

DGET New Delhi and CSTARI Kolkata have been implementing an annual pattern for all businesses in ITI since the August 2018 session. The examination system will also be changed and it will be online from this year and since all the questions are of Objective Type (MCQ), the trainees are in dire need of in-depth study. It is with this in mind that we are delighted to present the books based on the old NIMI pattern and a complete overview of the new annual pattern, and we hope that these books will be a guide for all business directors and trainees. Is.

For writing these books, Johar Awate Saheb, Principal of ITI Akluj. Former Principal of ITI Satara Saigavkar Saheb, Assistant Director Shri Chandrakant Dhekne Saheb Regional Office of Vocational Education and Training, Pune, District Vocational Education and Training Officer Sachin Dhumal Saheb and Headmaster Government Technical School Kendra Shalmali Pawar Madam and son Adhiraj Dole, mother Kusum Dole, I am very grateful to my father Madhukar Dole and wife Ashwini Dole for their special guidance and cooperation from time to time.

Also, in a very short period of time, the book was reviewed by Shri Rajendra Ghume Saheb, Joint Director, Vocational Education and Training Regional Office, Pune, for his invaluable time in publishing the book. I am sincerely grateful for their feedback.

I am grateful to the Instructor of ITI Satara for there continuous support from the very beginning of writing the book.

From this book, I consider myself blessed to have shared my thoughts on e-learning with you. I will not claim that this book is perfect, because considering the perfection, this book is an attempt and is in its infancy. They will be valuable for improvement if they are tested and suggested.

Manoj Dole
Dated 9/1/2019

Acknowledgements

The industrial training and theoretical examination system of our industrial training institutes and these changes have been accepted by the craft instructors and the trainees. Theoretical examinations conducted in your industrial training institutes are also conducted online. Since these examinations are of multiple choice MCQ method, the trainees will need to get more practice of such questions.

With all these considerations in mind, Mr. Manoj Madhukar, Director, Dole Crafts, Katari Industrial Training Institute, Satara, has done a thorough study and with his diligent work and added his keen intellect, according to the new annual system and NSQF-5 syllabus, e-book of Katari and other machine trades. -Book) and they have created mobile apps and blogs on theoretical topics to make training easier and have made all these educational materials available for download on the world famous websites Google Play Store, Amazon and Apple Book Store. Training has been made easier by creating a print version and using advanced techniques like QR Code.

All these educational materials will definitely be a guide for all the trainees for in-depth study and for the craft instructors and other concerned who are imparting vocational training.

CHAPTER ONE

Wireman Second Year QR Code Images

Download App
Online Test Exam
ITI Books
AutoCAD CAM
JOB & Apprentice
Online Theory
Computer Course
Trading Course
CNC Course
MSCIT Course
Shopping Business
Internet Business
Web Designing
Online Services
Top Sportsmans
Indian Army
Freedom Fighters
Top Scientists
Social Reformers
Motivational Speaker
Top Richest People
Join WhatsApp Group
Join Facebook Group
Like Facebook Page
PAN / Adhar / Licence Passport

18 ITI Book MCQ - Manoj Dole
www.itibook.com
battery
capacitor
cell
dynamometer
electromagnet
heater
inductance
magnet
www.itigov.blogspot.com www.jobapprentices.blogspot.com www.ititests.blogspot.com
www.itibook.com

15 ITI Book MCQ - Manoj Dole
www.itibook.com
megger
motor
multimeter
ohmmeter
resistores
star connected
alternator
voltmeter
ammeter
wattmeter
www.itigov.blogspot.com www.jobapprentices.blogspot.com www.ititests.blogspot.com
www.itibook.com

Coffee maker
Blender
Mixer
Toaster
Microwave
Crock pot
Rice cooker
Pressure cooker
Bachelor griller (U.K.)
Stove
Lamp
Light bulb
Lantern
Torch
Clothes iron
Electric drill

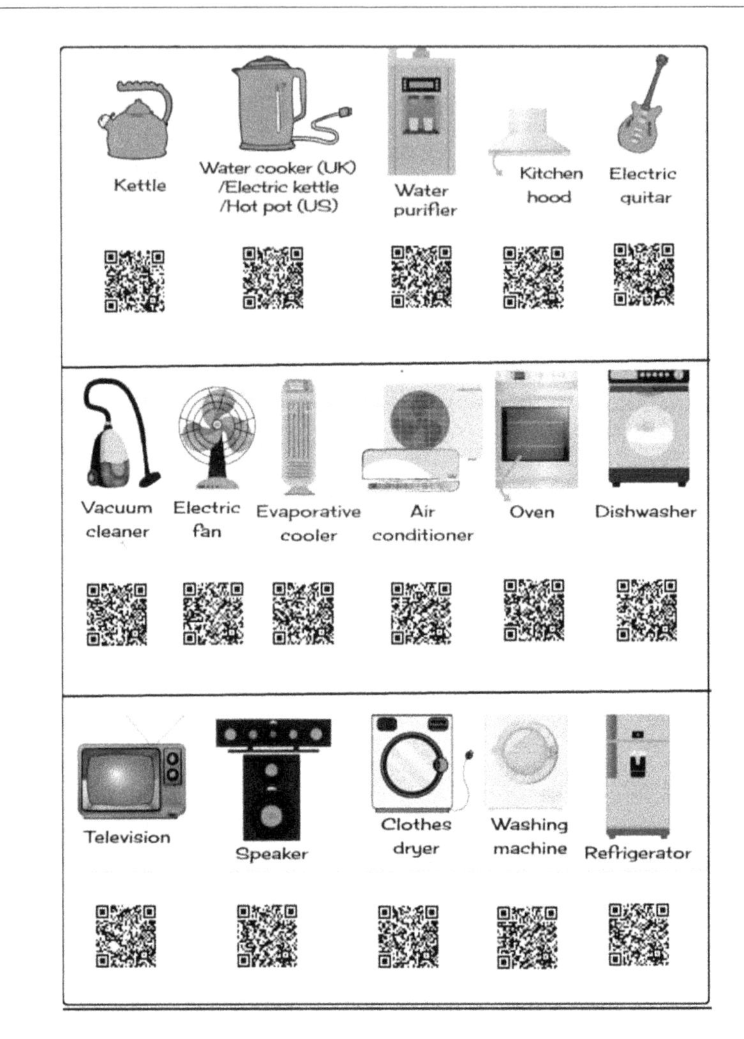
Kettle
Water cooker (UK) /Electric kettle /Hot pot (US)
Water purifier
Kitchen hood
Electric guitar
Vacuum cleaner
Electric fan
Evaporative cooler
Air conditioner
Oven
Dishwasher
Television
Speaker
Clothes dryer
Washing machine
Refrigerator

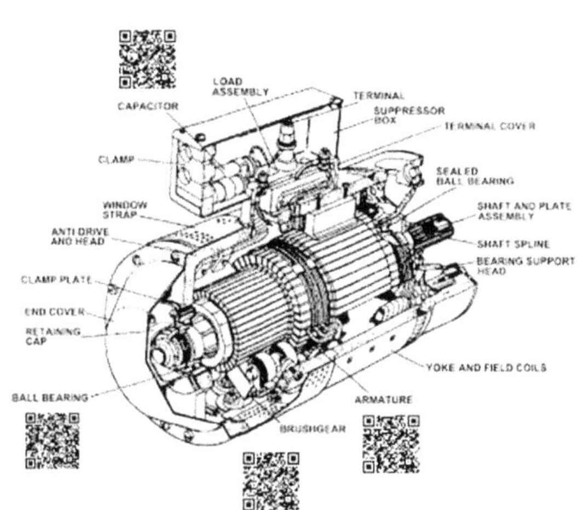

Electrical Generator

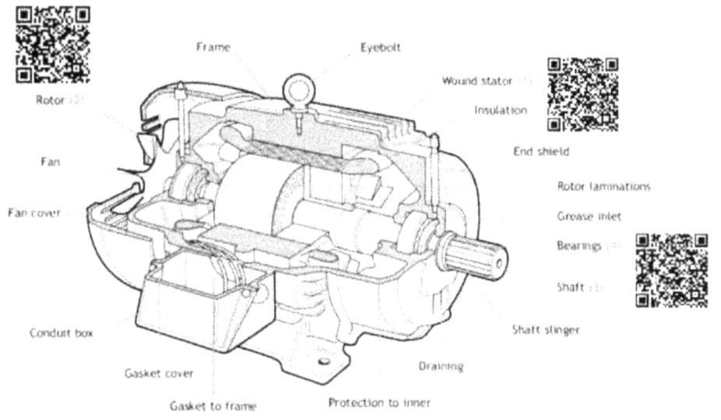

Electrical Induction Motor

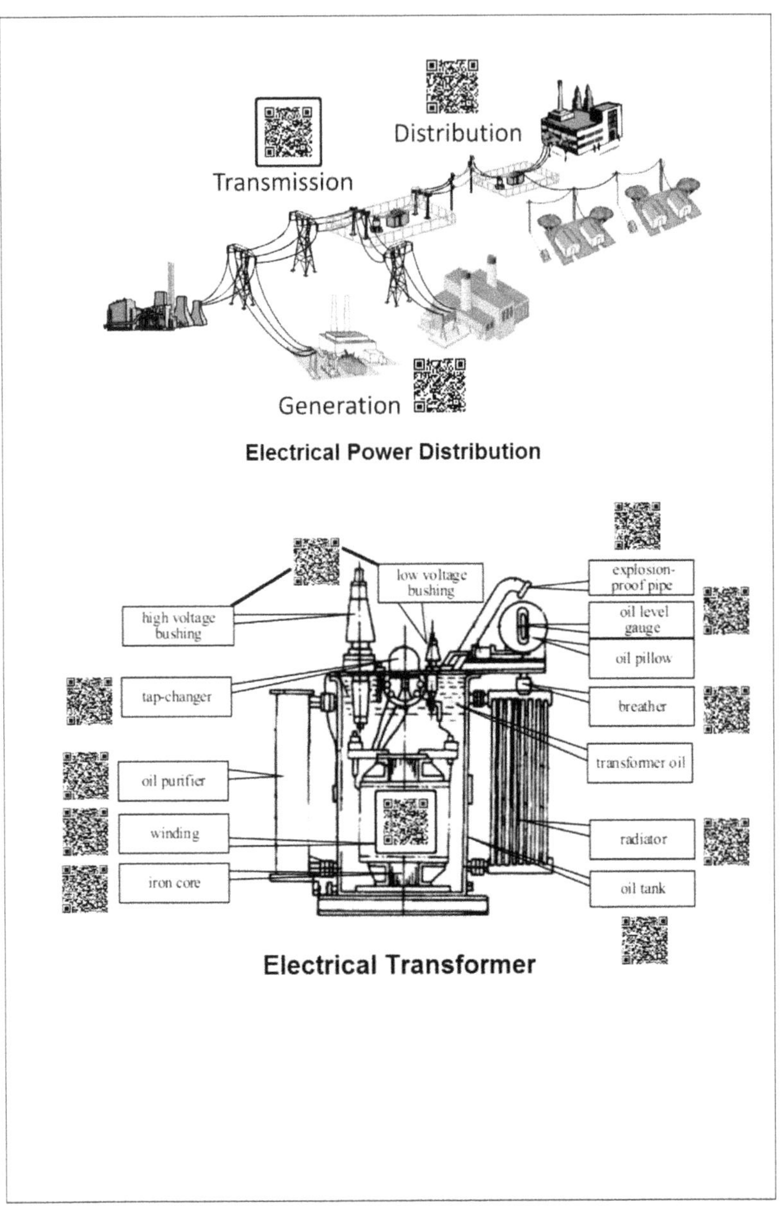

Electrical Power Distribution

Electrical Transformer

CHAPTER TWO

Wireman Second Year MCQ

1. A transistor has ....
A] one pn junction
B] two pn junctions
C] three pn junctions
D] four pn junctions
2. The number of depletion layers in a transistor is ....
A] four
B] three
C] one
D] two
3. The base of a transistor is .... doped
A] heavily
B] moderately
C] lightly
D] none of the above
4. The element that has the biggest size in a transistor is ....
A] collector
B] base
C] emitter
D] collector-base-junction
5. In a pnp transistor, the current carriers are ....
A] acceptor ions
B] donor ions
C] free electrons
D] holes
6. The collector of a transistor is .... doped
A] heavily
B] moderately

C] lightly
D] none of the above
7. A transistor is a .... operated device
A] current
B] voltage
C] both voltage and current
D] none of the above
8. In a npn transistor, ... are the minority carriers
A] free electrons
B] holes
C] donor ions
D] acceptor ions
9. The emitter of a transistor is .... doped
A] lightly
B] heavily
C] moderately
D] none of the above
10. In a transistor, the base current is about .... of emitter current
A] 25%
B] 20%
C] 35 %
D] 5%
11. At the base-emitter junctions of a transistor, one finds ....
A] a reverse bias
B] a wide depletion layer
C] low resistance
D] none of the above
12. The input impedance of a transistor is ....
A] high
B] low
C] very high
D] almost zero
13. Most of the majority carriers from the emitter ....
A] recombine in the base
B] recombine in the emitter
C] pass through the base region to the collector
D] none of the above
14. The current IB is ....

A] electron current
B] hole current
C] donor ion current
D] acceptor ion current
15. In a transistor ....
A] IC = IE + IB
B] IB = IC + IE
C] IE = IC – IB
D] IE = IC + IB
16. The value of a of a transistor is ....
A] more than 1
B] less than 1
C] 1
D] none of the above
17. IC = aIE + ...
A] IB
B] ICEO
C] ICBO
D] ßIB
18. The output impedance of a transistor is ....
A] high
B] zero
C] low
D] very low
19. In a tansistor, IC = 100 mA and IE = 100.2 mA. The value of ß is ....
A] 100
B] 50
C] about 1
D] 200
20. In a transistor if ß = 100 and collector current is 10 mA, then IE is ....
A] 100 mA
B] 100.1 mA
C] 110 mA
D] none of the above
21. The relation between ß and a is ....
A] ß = 1 / (1 – a)

B] ß = (1 – a) / a

C] ß = a / (1 – a)

D] ß = a / (1 + a)

22. The value of ß for a transistor is generally ....

A] 1less than 1

B] between 20 and 500

C] above 500

23. The most commonly used transistor arrangement is .... arrangement

A] common emitter

B] common base

C] common collector

D] none of the above

24. The input impedance of a transistor connected in ....arrangement is the highest

A] common emitter

B] common collector

C] common base

D] none of the above

25. The output impedance of a transistor connected in ....

A] arrangement is the highest

B] common emitter

C] common collector

D] common base

none of the above

26. The phase difference between the input and output voltages in a common base arrangement is ....

A] 180o

B] 90o

C] 270o

D] 0o

27. The power gain in a transistor connected in .... arrangement is the highest

A] common emitter

B] common base

C] common collector

D] none of the above

28. The phase difference between the input and output voltages of a

transistor connected in common emitter arrangement is ....

A] 0o

B] 180o

C] 90o

D] 270o

29. The voltage gain in a transistor connected in .... arrangement is the highest

A] common base

B] common collector

C] common emitter

D] none of the above

30. As the temperature of a transistor goes up, the base-emitter resistance ....

A] decreases

B] increases

C] remains the same

D] none of the above

31. The voltage gain of a transistor connected in common collector

A] arrangement is ....

B] equal to 1

C] more than 10

D] more than 100 less than 1

32. The phase difference between the input and output voltages of a transistor connected in common collector arrangement is ....

A] 180o

B] 0o

C] 90o

D] 270o

33. IC = ß IB + ...

A] ICBO

B] IC

C] ICEO

D] aIE

34. IC = [a / (1 – a)] IB + ...

A] ICEO

B] ICBO

C] IC

D] (1 – a) IB

35. IC = [a / (1 – a)] IB + [........ / (1 – a)]
A] ICBO
B] ICEO
C] IC
D] IE
36. BC 147 transistor indicates that it is made of ....
A] germanium
B] silicon
C] carbon
D] none of the above
37. ICEO = (.........) ICBO
A] ß1
B] + a
C] 1 + ß
D] none of the above
38. A transistor is connected in CB mode. If it is not connected in CE mode with same bias voltages, the values of IE, IB and IC will ....
A] remain the same
B] increase
C] decrease
D] none of the above
39. If the value of a is 0.9, then value of ß is ....
A] 9
B] 0.9
C] 900
D] 90
40. In a transistor, signal is transferred from a .... circuit
A] high resistance to low resistance
B] low resistance to high resistance
C] high resistance to high resistance
D] low resistance to low resistance
41. The arrow in the symbol of a transistor indicates the direction of ....
A] electron current in the emitter
B] electron current in the collector
C] hole current in the emitter
D] donor ion current

42. The leakage current in CE arrangement is .... that in CB arrangement

A] more than

B] less than

C] the same as

D] none of the above

43. A heat sink is generally used with a transistor to ....

A] increase the forward current

B] decrease the forward current

C] compensate for excessive doping

D] prevent excessive temperature rise

44. The most commonly used semiconductor in the manufacture of a transistor is ....

A] germanium

B] silicon

C] carbon

D] none of the above

45. The collector-base junction in a transistor has ....

A] forward bias at all times

B] reverse bias at all times

C] low resistance

D] none of the above

1. Transistor biasing represents .... conditions

1. a.c.

2. d.c.

3. both a.c. and d.c.

4. none of the above

Ans : 2

2. Transistor biasing is done to keep .... in the circuit

Proper direct current

Proper alternating current

The base current small

Collector current small

Ans : 1

3. Operating point represents ....

Values of IC and VCE when signal is applied

The magnitude of signal

Zero signal values of IC and VCE

None of the above
Ans : 3
TRANSISTOR BIASING Questions and Answers pdf
4. If biasing is not done in an amplifier circuit, it results in ....
Decrease in the base current
Unfaithful amplification
Excessive collector bias
None of the above
Ans : 2
5. Transistor biasing is generally provided by a ....
Biasing circuit
Bias battery
Diode
None of the above
Ans : 1
6. For faithful amplification by a transistor circuit, the value of VBE should .... for a silicon transistor
Be zero
Be 0.01 V
Not fall below 0.7 V
Be between 0 V and 0.1 V
Ans : 3
7. For proper operation of the transistor, its collector should have ....
Proper forward bias
Proper reverse bias
Very small size
None of the above
Ans : 2
8. For faithful amplification by a transistor circuit, the value of VCE should .... for silicon transistor
Not fall below 1 V
Be zero
Be 0.2 V
None of the above
Ans : 1
9. The circuit that provides the best stabilization of operating point is ....

Base resistor bias
Collector feedback bias
Potential divider bias
None of the above
Ans : 3
10. The point of intersection of d.c. and a.c. load lines represents ....
Operating point
Current gain
Voltage gain
None of the above
Ans : 1
11. An ideal value of stability factor is ....
100
200
More than 200
1
Ans : 4
12. The zero signal IC is generally .... mA in the initial stages of a transistor amplifier
41
3
More than 10
Ans : 2
13. If the maximum collector current due to signal alone is 3 mA, then zero signal collector current should be at least equal to ....
6 mA
mA
3 mA
1 mA
Ans : 3
14. The disadvantage of base resistor method of transistor biasing is that it ....
Is complicated
Is sensitive to changes in ß
Provides high stability
None of the above
Ans : 2

15. The biasing circuit has a stability factor of 50. If due to temperature change, ICBO changes by 1 μA, then IC will change by …………

100 μA

25 μA

20 μA

50 μA

Ans : 4

16. For good stabilsation in voltage divider bias, the current I1 flowing through R1 and R2 should be equal to or greater than

10 IB

3 IB

2 IB

4 IB

Ans : 1

17. The leakage current in a silicon transistor is about ………… the leakage current in a germanium transistor

One hundredth

One tenth

One thousandth

One millionth

Ans : 3

18. The operating point is also called the ………….

Cut off point

Quiescent point

Saturation point

None of the above

Ans : 2

19. For proper amplification by a transistor circuit, the operating point should be located at the ………….. of the d.c. load line

The end point

Middle

The maximum current point

None of the above

Ans : 2

20. The operating point ………………… on the a.c. load line

Also line

Does not lie
May or may not lie
Data insufficient
Ans : 1
21. The disadvantage of voltage divider bias is that it has ....
High stability factor
Low base current
Many resistors
None of the above
Ans : 3
22. Thermal runaway occurs when ....
Collector is reverse biased
Transistor is not biased
Emitter is forward biased
Junction capacitance is high
Ans : 2
23. The purpose of resistance in the emitter circuit of a transistor amplifier is to ....
Limit the maximum emitter current
Provide base-emitter bias
Limit the change in emitter current
None of the above
Ans : 3
24. In a transistor amplifier circuit VCE = VCB + ...
VBE
2VBE
5 VBE
None of the above
Ans : 1
25. The base resistor method is generally used in ....
Amplifier circuits
Switching circuits
Rectifier circuits
None of the above
Ans : 2
26. For germanium transistor amplifier, VCE should .... for faithful amplification
Be zero

Be 0.2 V

Not fall below 0.7 V

None of the above

Ans : 3

27. In a base resistor method, if the value of ß changes by 50, then collector current will change by a factor ....

25

50

100

200

Ans : 2

28. The stability factor of a collector feedback bias circuit is .... that of base resistor bias.

The same as

More than

Less than

None of the above

Ans : 3

29. In the design of a biasing circuit, the value of collector load RC is determined by ....

VCE consideration

VBE consideration

IB consideration

None of the above

Ans : 1

30. If the value of collector current IC increases, then the value of VCE ....

Remains the same

Decreases

Increases

None of the above

Ans : 2

31. If the temperature increases, the value of VCE ....

Remains the same

Is increased

Is decreased

None of the above

Ans : 3

32. The stabilisation of operating point in potential divider method is provided by ....

RE consideration

RC consideration

VCC consideration

None of the above

Answer: 1

33. The value of VBE ....

Depends upon IC to moderate extent

Is almost independent of IC

Is strongly dependant on IC

None of the above

Ans : 2

34. When the temperature changes, the operating point is shifted due to ....

Change in ICBO

Change in VCC

Change in the values of circuit resistance

None of the above

Ans : 1

35. The value of stability factor for a base resistor bias is ....

RB (ß+1)

(ß+1)RC

(ß+1)

1-ß

Ans : 3

36. In a particular biasing circuit, the value of RE is about ....

10 kO

1 MO

100 kO

800 O

Ans : 4

37. A silicon transistor is biased with base resistor method. If ß=100, VBE =0.7 V, zero signal collector current IC = 1 mA and VCC = 6V , what is the value of the base resistor RB?

105 kO

530 kO

315 kO

None of the above

Ans : 2

38. In voltage divider bias, VCC = 25 V; R1 = 10 kO; R2 = 2.2 V ; RC = 3.6 V and RE =1 kO. What is the emitter voltage?

7 V

3 V

V8

V

Ans : 4

39. In the above question (Q38.) , what is the collector voltage?

3 V

8 V

6 V

7 V

Ans : 1

40. In voltage divider bias, operating point is 3 V, 2 mA. If VCC = 9 V, RC = 2.2 kO, what is the value of RE ?

2000 O

1400 O

800 O

1600 O

Ans : 3

1. A tuned amplifier uses .... load

A] Resistive

B] Capacitive

C] LC tank

D] Inductive

2. A tuned amplifier is generally operated in .... operation

A] Class A

B] Class C

C] Class B

D] None of the above

3. A tuned amplifier is used in .... applications

A] Radio frequency

B] Low frequency

C] Audio frequency

D] None of the above

4. Frequencies above .... kHz are called radio frequencies

A] 21
B] 0
C] 50
D] 200
6. The voltage gain of a tuned amplifier is .... at resonant frequency
A] Minimum
B] Maximum
C] Half-way between maximum and minimum
D] Zero
7. At parallel resonance, the line current is ....
A] Minimum
B] Maximum
C] Quite large
D] None of the above
8. At series resonance, the circuit offers .... impedance
A] Zero
B] Maximum
C] Minimum
D] None of the above
9. A resonant circuit contains .... elements
A] R and L only
B] R and C only
C] Only R
D] L and C
10. At series or parallel resonance, the circuit behaves as a .... load
A] Capacitive
B] Resistive
C] Inductive
D] None of the above
11. At series resonance, voltage across L is .... voltage across C
A] Equal to but opposite in phase to
B] Equal to but in phase with
C] Greater than but in phase with
D] Less than but in phase with
12. When either L or C is increased, the resonant frequency of LC circuit ....
A] Remains the same
B] Increases

C] Decreases

D] Insufficient data

13. At parallel resonance, the net reactive component circuit current is ………..

A] Capacitive

B] Zero

C] Inductive

D] None of the above

14. In parallel resonance, the circuit impedance is ………….

A] C/LR

B] R/LC

C] CR/L

D] L/CR

15. In a parallel LC circuit, if the input signal frequency is increased above resonant frequency then ……………………

A] XL increases and XC decreases

B] XL decreases and XC increases

C] Both XL and XC increase

D] Both XL and XC decrease

16. The Q of an LC circuit is given by …………………

A] 2pfr x R

B] R / 2pfrL

C] 2pfrL / R

D] R2/2pfrL

17. If Q of an LC circuit increases, then bandwidth …………………

A] Increases

B] Decreases

C] Remains the same

D] Insufficient data

18. At series resonance, the net reactive component of circuit current is ……………….

A] Zero

B] Inductive

C] Capacitive

D] None of the above

19. The dimensions of L/CR are that of ……………

A] Farad

B] Henry

C] Ohm

D] None of the above

20. If L/C ratio of a parallel LC circuit is increased, the Q of the circuit ....

A] Is decreased

B] Is increased

C] Remains the same

D] None of the above

21. At series resonance, the phase angle between applied voltage and circuit is ....

A] 90o

B] 180o

C] 0o

D] None of the above

22. At parallel resonance, the ratio L/C is ....

A] Very large

B] Zero

C] Small

D] None of the above

23. If the resistance of a tuned circuit is increased, the Q of the circuit ....

A] Is increased

B] Is decreased

C] Remains the same

D] None of the above

24. The Q of a tuned circuit refers to the property of ....

A] Sensitivity

B] Fidelity

C] Selectivity

D] None of the above

25. At parallel resonance, the phase angle between the applied voltage and circuit current is ....

A] 90o

B] 180o

C] 0o

D] None of the above

26. In a parallel LC circuit, if the signal frequency is decreased below the resonant frequency, then ....

A] XL decreases and XC increases
B] XL increases and XC decreases
C] Line current becomes minimum
D] None of the above

27. In series resonance, there is ....
A] Voltage amplification
B] Current amplification
C] Both voltage and current amplification
D] None of the above

28. The Q of a tuned amplifier is generally ....
A] Less than 5
B] Less than 10
C] More than 10
D] None of the above

29. The Q of a tuned amplifier is 50. If the resonant frequency for the amplifier is 1000kHZ, then bandwidth is ....
A] 10kHz
B] 40 kHz
C] 30 kHz
D] 20 kHz

30. In the above question, what are the values of cut-off frequencies?
A] 140 kHz , 60 kHz
B] 1020 kHz , 980 kHz
C] 1030 kHz , 970 kHz
D] None of the above

31. For frequencies above the resonant frequency, a parallel LC circuit behaves as a .... load
A] Capacitive
B] Resistive
C] Inductive
D] None of the above

32. In parallel resonance, there is ....
A] Both voltage and current amplification
B] Voltage amplifications
C] Current amplification
D] None of the above

33. For frequencies below resonant frequency, a series LC circuit behaves as a .... load

A] Resistive

B] Capacitive

C] Inductive

D] None of the above

34. If a high degree of selectivity is desired, then double-tuned circuit should have .... coupling

A] Loose

B] Tight

C] Critical

D] None of the above

35. In the double tuned circuit, if the mutual inductance between the two tuned circuits is decreased, the level of resonance curve ....

A] Remains the same

B] Is lowered

C] Is raised

D] None of the above

36. For frequencies above the resonant frequency , a series LC circuit behaves as a .... load

A] Resistive

B] Inductive

C] Capacitive

D] None of the above

37. Double tuned circuits are used in .... stages of a radio receiver

A] IF

B] Audio

C] Output

D] None of the above

38. A class C amplifier always drives .... load

A] A pure resistive

B] A pure inductive

C] A pure capacitive

D] A resonant tank

39. Tuned class C amplifiers are used for RF signals of ....

A] Low power

B] High power

C] Very high power

D] None of the above

40. For frequencies below the resonant frequency , a parallel LC circuit behaves as a .... load

A] Inductive

B] Resistive

C] Capacitive

D] None of the above

1. A radio receiver has .... of amplification

A] One stage

B] Two stages

C] Three stages

D] More than one stages

2. RC coupling is used for .... amplification

A] Voltage

B] Current

C] Power

D] None of the above

3. In an RC coupled amplifier, the voltage gain over mid-frequency range ....

A] Changes abruptly with frequency

B] Is constant

C] Changes uniformly with frequency

D] None of the above

4. In obtaining the frequency response curve of an amplifier, the ....

A] Amplifier level output is kept constant

B] Amplifier frequency is held constant

C] Generator frequency is held constant

D] Generator output level is held constant

5. An advantage of RC coupling scheme is the ....Good impedance matching

A] Economy

B] High efficiency

C] None of the above

6. The best frequency response is of .... coupling

A] RC

B] Transformer

C] Direct

D] None of the above

7. Transformer coupling is used for .... amplification

A] Power

B] Voltage

C] Current

D] None of the above

8. In an RC coupling scheme, the coupling capacitor CC must be large enough ....

A] To pass d.c. between the stages

B] Not to attenuate the low frequencies

C] To dissipate high power

D] None of the above

9. In RC coupling, the value of coupling capacitor is about ....

A] 100 pF

B] 0.1 μF

C] 0.01 μF

D] 10 μF

11. When a multistage amplifier is to amplify d.c. signal, then one must use .... coupling

A] RC

B] Transformer

C] Direct

D] None of the above

12. .... coupling provides the maximum voltage gain

A] RC

B] Transformer

C] Direct

D] Impedance

13. In practice, voltage gain is expressed ....

A] In db

B] In volts

C] As a number

D] None of the above

14. Transformer coupling provides high efficiency because ....

A] Collector voltage is stepped up

B] resistance is low

C] collector voltage is stepped down

D] none of the above

15. Transformer coupling is generally employed when load resistance is ....

A] Large
B] Very large
C] Small
D] None of the above

16. If a three-stage amplifier has individual stage gains of 10 db, 5 db and 12 db, then total gain in db is ....
A] 600 db
B] 24 db
C] 14 db
D] 27 db

17. The final stage of a multistage amplifier uses ....
A] RC coupling
B] Transformer coupling
C] Direct coupling
D] Impedance coupling

18. The ear is not sensitive to ....
A] Frequency distortion
B] Amplitude distortion
C] Frequency as well as amplitude distortion
D] None of the above

19. RC coupling is not used to amplify extremely low frequencies because ....
A] There is considerable power loss
B] There is hum in the output
C] Electrical size of coupling capacitor becomes very large
D] None of the above

20. In transistor amplifiers, we use .... transformer for impedance matching
A] Step up
B] Step down
C] Same turn ratio
D] None of the above

21. The lower and upper cut off frequencies are also called .... frequencies
A] Sideband
B] Resonant
C] Half-resonant
D] Half-power

22. A gain of 1,000,000 times in power is expressed by ....
A] 30 db
B] <u>60 db</u>
C] 120 db
D] 600 db
23. A gain of 1000 times in voltage is expressed by ....
A] <u>60 db</u>
B] 30 db
C] 120 db
D] 600 db
24. 1 db corresponds to .... change in power level
A] 50%
B] 35%
C] <u>26%</u>
D] 22%
25. 1 db corresponds to .... change in voltage or current level
A] <u>40%</u>
B] 80%
C] 20%
D] 25%
26. The frequency response of transformer coupling is ....
A] Good
B] Very good
C] Excellent
D] <u>Poor</u>
27. In the initial stages of a multistage amplifier, we use ....
A] <u>RC coupling</u>
B] Transformer coupling
C] Direct coupling
D] None of the above
28. The total gain of a multistage amplifier is less than the product of the gains of individual stages due to ....
A] Power loss in the coupling device
B] <u>Loading effect of the next stage</u>
C] The use of many transistors
D] The use of many capacitors
29. The gain of an amplifier is expressed in db because ....
A] It is a simple unit

B] Calculations become easy

C] Human ear response is logarithmic

D] None of the above

30. If the power level of an amplifier reduces to half, the db gain will fall by ....

A] 5 db

B] 2 db

C] 10 db

D] 3 db

31. A current amplification of 2000 is a gain of ....

A] 3 db

B] 66 db

C] 20 db

D] 200 db

32. An amplifier receives 0.1 W of input signal and delivers 15 W of signal power. What is the power gain in db?

A] 8 db

B] 6 db

C] 5 db

D] 4 db

33. The power output of an audio system is 18 W. For a person to notice an increase in the output (loudness or sound intensity) of the system, what must the output power be increased to ?

A] 2 W

B] 6 W

C] 68 W

D] None of the above

34. The output of a microphone is rated at -52 db. The reference level is 1V under specified conditions. What is the output voltage of this microphone under the same sound conditions?

A] 5 mV

B] 2 mV

C] 8 mV

D] 5 mV

35. RC coupling is generally confined to low power applications because of ....

A] Large value of coupling capacitor

B] Low efficiency

C] Large number of components

D] None of the above

36. The number of stages that can be directly coupled is limited because ....

A] Changes in temperature cause thermal instability

B] Circuit becomes heavy and costly

C] It becomes difficult to bias the circuit

D] None of the above

37. The purpose of RC or transformer coupling is to ....

A] Block a.c.

B] Separate bias of one stage from another

C] Increase thermal stability

D] None of the above

38. The upper or lower cut off frequency is also called ....frequency

A] Resonant

B] Sideband

C] 3 db

D] None of the above

39. The bandwidth of a single stage amplifier is .... that of a multistage amplifier

A] More than

B] The same as

C] Less than

D] Data insufficient

40. The value of emitter capacitor CE in a multistage amplifier is about ....

A] 1 μF

B] 100 pF

C] 0.01 μF

D] 50 μF

1. Laminations of core are generally made of

(a) case iron

(b) carbon

(c) silicon steel

(d) stainless steel

2. Which of the following could be lamina-proximately the thickness of laminations of a D.C. machine ?

(a) 0.005 mm

(b) 0.05 mm
(c) 0.5 m
(d) 5 m

3. The armature of D.C. generator is laminated to
(a) reduce the bulk
(b) provide the bulk
(c) insulate the core
(d) reduce eddy current loss

4. The resistance of armature winding depends on
(a) length of conductor
(b) cross-sectional area of the conductor
(c) number of conductors
(d) all of the above

5. The field coils of D.C. generator are usually made of
(a) mica
(b) copper
(c) cast iron
(d) carbon

6. The commutator segments are connected to the armature conductors by means of
(a) copper lugs
(b) resistance wires
(c) insulation pads
(d) brazing

7. In a commutator
(a) copper is harder than mica
(b) mica and copper are equally hard
(c) mica is harder than copper
(d) none of the above

8. In D.C. generators the pole shoes are fastened to the pole core by
(a) rivets
(b) counter sunk screws
(c) brazing
(d) welding

9. According to Fleming's right-hand rule for finding the direction of induced e.m.f., when middle finger points in the direction of induced e.m.f., forefinger will point in the direction of
(a) motion of conductor

(b) lines of force

(c) either of the above

(d) none of the above

10. Fleming's right-hand rule regarding direction of induced e.m.f., correlates

(a) magnetic flux, direction of current flow and resultant force

(b) magnetic flux, direction of motion and the direction of e.m.f. induced

(c) magnetic field strength, induced voltage and current

(d) magnetic flux, direction of force and direction of motion of conductor

11. While applying Fleming's right-hand rule to And the direction of induced e.m.f., the thumb points towards

(a) direction of induced e.m.f.

(b) direction of flux

(c) direction of motion of the conductor if forefinger points in the direction of generated e.m.f.

(d) direction of motion of conductor, if forefinger points along the lines of flux

12. The bearings used to support the rotor shafts are generally

(a) ball bearings

(b) bush bearings

(c) magnetic bearmgs

(d) needle bearings

13. In D.C. generators, the cause of rapid brush wear may be

(a) severe sparking

(b) rough commutator surface

(c) imperfect contact

(d) any of the above

14. In lap winding, the number of brushes is always

(a) double the number of poles

(b) same as the number of poles

(c) half the number of poles

(d) two

15. For a D.C. generator when the number of poles and the number of armature conductors is fixed, then which winding will give the higher e.m.f. ?

(a) Lap winding

(b) <u>Wave winding</u>
(c) Either of (a) and (b) above
(d) Depends on other features of design
16. In a four-pole D.C. machine
(a) all the four poles are north poles
(b) <u>alternate poles are north and south</u>
(c) all the four poles are south poles
(d) two north poles follow two south poles
17. Copper brushes in D.C. machine are used
(a) <u>where low voltage and high currents are involved</u>
(b) where high voltage and small cur-rents are involved
(c) in both of the above cases
(d) in none of the above cases
18. A separately excited generator as compared to a self-excited generator
(a) is amenable to better voltage control
(b) is more stable
(c) has exciting current independent of load current
(d) <u>has all above features</u>
19. In case of D.C. machines, mechanical losses are primary function of
(a) current
(b) voltage
(c) <u>speed</u>
(d) none of above
20. Iron losses in a D.C. machine are independent of variations in
(a) speed
(b) <u>load</u>
(c) voltage
(d) speed and voltage
21. In D.C. generators, current to the external circuit from armature is given through
(a) <u>commutator</u>
(b) solid connection
(c) slip rings
(d) none of above
23. Brushes of D.C. machines are made of
(a) <u>carbon</u>
(b) soft copper

(c) hard copper
(d) all of above

24. If B is the flux density, I the length of conductor and v the velocity of conductor, then induced e.m.f. is given by
(a)Blv
(b)Blv2
(c)Bl2v
(d)Bl2v2

25. In case of a 4-pole D.C. generator provided with a two layer lap winding with sixteen coils, the pole pitch will be
(a) 4
(b) 8
(c) 16
(d) 32

26. The material for commutator brushes is generally
(a) mica
(b) copper
(c) cast iron
(d) carbon

27. The insulating material used between the commutator segments is normally
(a) graphite
(b) paper
(c) mica
(d) insulating varnish

28. In D.C. generators, the brushes on commutator remain in contact with conductors which
(a) lie under south pole
(b) lie under north pole
(c) lie under interpolar region
(d) are farthest from the poles

29. If brushes of a D.C. generator are moved in order to bring these brushes in
magnetic neutral axis, there will be
(a) demagnetisation only
(b) cross magnetisation as well as mag¬netisation
(c) crossmagnetisation as well as demagnetising
(d) cross magnetisation only

30. Armature reaction of an unsaturated D.C. machine is

(a) crossmagnetising

(b) demagnetising

(c) magnetising

(d) none of above

31. D.C. generators are connected to the busbars or disconnected from them only under the floating condition

(a) to avoid sudden loading of the primemover

(b) to avoid mechanicaljerk to the shaft

(c) to avoid burning of switch contacts

(d) all above

32. Eddy currents are induced in the pole shoes of a D.C. machine due to

(a) oscillating magnetic field

(b) pulsating magnetic flux

(c) relative rotation between field and armature

(d) all above

34. Equilizer rings are required in case armature is

(a) wave wound

(b) lap wound

(c) delta wound

(d) duplex wound

35. Welding generator will have

(a) lap winding

(b) wave winding

(c) delta winding

(d) duplex wave winding

36. In case of D.C. machine winding, number of commutator segments is equal to

(a) number of armature coils

(b) number of armature coil sides

(c) number of armature conductors

(d) number of armature turns

37. For a D.C. machines laboratory following type of D.C. supply will be suitable

(a) rotary converter

(b) mercury are rectifier

(c) induction motor D.C. generator set

(d) synchronous motor D.C. generator set

38. The function of pole shoes in the case of D.C. machine is

(a) to reduce the reluctance of the mag¬netic path

(b) to spread out the flux to achieve uniform flux density

(c) to support the field coil

(d) to discharge all the above functions

Ans: d

39. In the case of lap winding resultant pitch is

(a) multiplication of front and back pitches

(b) division of front pitch by back pitch

(c) sum of front and back pitches

(d) difference of front and back pitches

40. A D.C. welding generator has

(a) lap winding

(b) wave moving

(c) duplex winding

(d) any of the above

41. Which of the following statement about D.C. generators is false ?

(a) Compensating winding in a D.C. machine helps in commutation

(b) In a D. C. generator interpoles winding is connected in series with the armature winding

(c) Back pitch and front pitch are both odd and approximately equal to the pole pitch

(d) Equilizing bus bars are used with parallel running of D.C. shunt generators

42. The demagnetising component of armature reaction in a D.C. generator

(a) reduces generator e.m.f.

(b) increases armature speed

(c) reduces interpoles flux density

(d) results in sparking trouble

43. Magnetic field in a D.C. generator is produced by

(a) electromagnets

(b) permanent magnets

(c) both (a) and (b)

(d) none of the above

44. The number of brushes in a commutator depends on

(a) speed of armature

(b) type of winding

(c) voltage

(d) amount of current to be collected

45. Compensating windings are used in D.C. generators

(a) mainly to reduce the eddy currents by providing local short-circuits

(b) to provide path for the circulation of cooling air

(c) to neutralise the cross-magnetising effect of the armature reaction

(d) none of the above

46. Which of the following components of a D.C, generator plays vital role for

providing direct current of a D.C. generator ?

(a) Dummy coils

(b) Commutator

(c) Eye bolt

(d) Equilizer rings

47. In a D.C. generator the ripples in the direct e.m.f. generated are reduced by

(a) using conductor of annealed copper

(b) using commutator with large number of segments

(c) using carbon brushes of superior quality

(d) using equiliser rings

48. In D.C. generators, lap winding is used for

(a) high voltage, high current

(b) low voltage, high current

(c) high voltage, low current

(d) low voltage, low current

49. Two generators A and B have 6-poles each. Generator A has wave wound armature while generator B has lap wound armature. The ratio of the induced e.m.f. is generator A and B will be

(a) 2 : 3

(b) 3 : 1

(c) 3 : 2

(d) 1 : 3

50. The voltage drop for which of the following types of brush can be expected to be least ?

(a) Graphite brushes

(b) Carbon brushes

(c) Metal graphite brushes

(d) None of the above

51. The e.m.f. generated by a shunt wound D.C. generator isE. Now while pole flux remains constant, if the speed of the generator is doubled, the e.m.f. generated will be

(a) E/2

(b) 2E

(c) slightly less than E

(d) E

53. The armature core of a D.C. generator is usually made of

(a) silicon steel

(b) copper

(c) non-ferrous material

(d) cast-iron

54. Satisfactory commutation of D.C. machines requires

(a) brushes should be of proper grade and size

(b) brushes should smoothly run in the holders

(c) smooth, concentric commutator properly undercut

(d) all of the above

54a. Open circuited armature coil of a D.C. machine is

(a) identified by the scarring of the commutator segment to which open circuited coil is connected

(b) indicated by a spark completely around the commutator

(c) both (a) and (b)

(d) none of the above

56. For the parallel operation of two or more D.C. compound generators, we

should ensure that

(a) voltage of the incoming generator should be same as that of bus bar

(b) polarity of incoming generator should be same as that of bus bar

(c) all the series fields should be run in parallel by means of equilizer connection

(d) series fields of all generators should be either on positive side or negative side of the armature

57. D.C. series generator is used

(a) to supply traction load

(b) to supply industrial load at constant voltage

(c) voltage at the toad end of the feeder

(d) for none of the above purpose

58. Following D.C. generator will be in a position to build up without any residual magnetism in the poles

(a) series generator

(b) shunt generator

(c) compound generator

(d) self-excited generator

59. Interpole flux should be sufficient to

(a) neutralise the commutating self induced e.m.f.

(b) neutralise the armature reaction flux

(c) neutralise both the armature reaction flux as well as commutating e.m.f. induced in the coil

(d) perform none of the above functions

60. D.C. generator generally preferred for charging automobile batteries is

(a) series generator

(b) shunt generator

(c) long shunt compound generator

(d) any of'the above

61. In a D.C. generator the number of mechanical degrees and electrical degrees will be the same when

(a) r.p.m. is more than 300

(b) r.p.m. is less than 300

(c) number of poles is 4

(d) number of poles is 2

62. Permeance is the reciprocal of

(a) flux density

(b) reluctance

(c) ampere-turns

(d) resistance

63. In D.C. generators the polarity of the interpoles

(a) is the same as that of the main pole ahead

(b) is the same as that of the immediately preceding pole

(c) is opposite to that of the main pole ahead

(d) is neutral as these poles do not play part in generating e.m.f.

64. The e.m.f. generated in a D.C. generator is directly proportional to

(a) flux/pole

(b) speed of armature

(c) number of poles

(d) all of the above

65. In a D.C. generator the magnetic neutral axis coincides with the geometrical neutral axis, when

(a) there is no load on|he generator

(b) the generator runs on full load

(c) the generator runs on overload

(d) the generator runs on designed speed

66. In a D.C. generator in order to reduce sparking at brushes, the self-induced e.m.f. in the coil is neutralised by all of the following except

(a) interpoles

(b) dummy coils

(c) compensating winding

(d) shifting of axis of brushes

67. In D.C. generators on no-load, the air gap flux distribution in space is

(a) sinusoidal

(b) triangular

(c) pulsating

(d) flat topped

68. A shunt generator running at 1000 r.p.m. has generated e.m.f. as 200 V. If the speed increases to 1200 r.p.m., the generated e.m.f. will be nearly

(a) 150 V

(b) 175 V

(c) 240 V

(d) 290 V

69. The purpose of providing dummy coils in a generator is

(a) to reduce eddy current losses

(b) to enhance flux density

(c) to amplify voltage

(d) to provide mechanical balance for the rotor

1. No-load speed of which of the following motor will be highest ?

(a) Shunt motor

(b) Series motor

(c) Cumulative compound motor

(d) Differentiate compound motor

2. The direction of rotation of a D.C. series motor can be changed by

(a) interchanging supply terminals

(b) interchanging field terminals

(c) either of (a) and (b) above

(d) None of the above

3. Which of the following application requires high starting torque ?

(a) Lathe machine

(b) Centrifugal pump

(c) Locomotive

(d) Air blower

4. If a D.C. motor is to be selected for conveyors, which rriotor would be preferred ?

(a) Series motor

(b) Shunt motor

(c) Differentially compound motor

(d) Cumulative compound motor

5. Which D.C. motor will be preferred for machine tools ?

(a) Series motor

(b) Shunt motor

(c) Cumulative compound motor

(d) Differential compound motor

6. Differentially compound D.C. motors can find applications requiring

(a) high starting torque

(b) low starting torque

(c) variable speed

(d) frequent on-off cycles

7. Which D.C. motor is preferred for elevators ?

(a) Shunt motor

(b) Series motor

(c) Differential compound motor

(d) Cumulative compound motor

8. According to Fleming's left-hand rule, when the forefinger points in the direction of the field or flux, the middle finger will point in the direction of

(a) current in the conductor aovtaat of conductor

(c) resultant force on conductor

(d) none of the above

9. If the field of a D.C. shunt motor gets opened while motor is running

(a) the speed of motor will be reduced %

(b) the armature current will reduce

(c) the motor will attain dangerously high speed 1

(d) the motor will continue to nuvat constant speed

10. Starters are used with D.C. motors because
(a) these motors have high starting torque
(b) these motors are not self-starting
(c) back e.m.f. of these motors is zero initially
(d) to restrict armature current as there is no back e.m.f. while starting
11. In D.C. shunt motors as load is reduced
(a) the speed will increase abruptly
(b) the speed will increase in proportion to reduction in load
(c) the speed will remain almost/constant
(d) the speed will reduce
12. A D.C. series motor is that which
(a) has its field winding consisting of thick wire and less turns
(b) has a poor torque
(c) can be started easily without load
(d) has almost constant speed
13. For starting a D.C. motor a starter is required because
(a) it limits the speed of the motor
(b) it limits the starting current to a safe value
(c) it starts the motor
(d) none of the above
14. The type of D.C. motor used for shears and punches is
(a) shunt motor
(b) series motor
(c) differential compoutid D.C. motor
(d) cumulative compound D.C. motor
15. If a D.C. motor is connected across the A.C. supply it will
(a) run at normal speed
(b) not run
(c) run at lower speed
(d) burn due to heat produced in the field winding by .eddy currents
16. To get the speed of D.C, motor below the normal without wastage of electrical energy is used.
(a) Ward Leonard control
(b) rheostatic control
(c) any of the above method
(d) none of the above method
17. When two D.C. series motors are connected in parallel, the resultant speed is

(a) more than the normal speed
(b) loss than the normal speed
(c) normal speed
(d) zero

18. The speed of a D.C. shunt motor more than its full-load speed can be obtained by
(a) decreasing the field current
(b) increasing the field current
(c) decreasing the armature current
(d) increasing the armature current

19. In a D.C. shunt motor, speed is
(a) independent of armature current
(b) directly proportional to the armature current
(c) proportional to the square of the current
(d) inversely proportional to the armature current

20. A direct on line starter is used: for starting motors
(a) up to 5 H.P.
(b) up to 10 H.P.
(c) up to 15 H.P.
(d) up to 20 H.P.

21. What will happen if the back e.m.f. of a D.C. motor vanishes suddenly?
(a) The motor will stop
(b) The motor will continue to run
(c) The armature may burn
(d) The motor will run noisy

22. In case of D.C. shunt motors the speed is dependent on back e.m.f. only because
(a) back e.m.f. is equal to armature drop
(b) armature drop is negligible
(c) flux is proportional to armature current
(d) flux is practically constant in D:C. shunt motors

23. In a D.C. shunt motor, under the conditions of maximum power, the current in the armature will be
(a) almost negligible
(b) rated full-load current
(c) less than full-load current
(d) more than full-load current

24. These days D.C. motors are widely used in
(a) pumping sets
(b) air compressors
(c) electric traction
(d) machine shops

25. By looking at which part of the motor, it can be easily confirmed that a particular motor is D.C. motor?
(a) Frame
(b) Shaft
(c) Commutator
(d) Stator

26. In which of the following applications D.C. series motor is invariably tried?
(a) Starter for a car
(b) Drive for a water pump
(c) Fan motor
(d) Motor operation in A.C. or D.C.

27. In D.C. machines fractional pitch winding is used
(a) to improve cooling
(b) to reduce copper losses
(c) to increase the generated e.m.f.
(d) to reduce the sparking

28. A three point starter is considered suitable for
(a) shunt motors
(b) shunt as well as compound motors
(c) shunt, compound and series motors
(d) all D.C. motors

29. In case-the conditions for maximum power for a D.C. motor are established, the efficiency of the motor will be
(a) 100%
(b) around 90%
(c) anywhere between 75% and 90%
(d) less than 50%

30. The ratio of starting torque to full-load torque is least in case of
(a) series motors
(b) shunt motors
(c) compound motors
(d) none of the above

31. In D.C. motor which of the following can sustain the maximum temperature rise?

(a) Slip rings

(b) Commutator

(c) Field winding

(d) Armature winding

33. Which of the following law/rule can he used to determine the direction of rotation of D.C. motor ?

(a) Lenz's law

(b) Faraday's law

(c) Coloumb's law

(d) Fleming's left-hand rule

34. Which of the following load normally needs starting torque more than the rated torque?

(a) Blowers

(b) Conveyors

(c) Air compressors

(d) Centrifugal pumps

35. The starting resistance of a D.C. motor is generally

(a) low

(b) around 500 Q

(c) 1000 Q

(d) infinitely large

36. The speed of a D.C. series motor is

(a) proportional to the armature current

(b) proportional to the square of the armature current

(c) proportional to field current

(d) inversely proportional to the armature current

37. In a D.C. series motor, if the armature current is reduced by 50%, the torque of the motor will be equal to

(a) 100% of the previous value

(b) 50% of the previous value

(c) 25% of the previous value

(d) 10% of the previous value

38. The current drawn by the armature of D.C. motor is directly proportional to

(a) the torque required

(b) the speed of the motor

(c) the voltage across the terminals

(d) none of the above

39. The power mentioned on the name plate of an electric motor indicates

(a) the power drawn in kW

(b) the power drawn in kVA

(c) the gross power

(d) the output power available at the shaft

40. Which D.C. motor has got maximum self loading property?

(a) Series motor

(b) Shunt motor

(c) Cumulatively compounded ‘motor

(d) Differentially compounded motor

41. Which D.C. motor will be suitable along with flywheel for intermittent light and heavy loads?

(a) Series motor

(b) Shunt motor

(c) Cumulatively compounded motor

(d) Differentially compounded motor

42. If a D.C. shunt motor is working at no load and if shunt field circuit suddenly opens

(a) nothing will happen to the motor

(b) this will make armature to take heavy current, possibly burning it

(c) this will result in excessive speed, possibly destroying armature due to excessive centrifugal stresses

(d) motor will run at very slow speed

43. D.C. series motors are used

(a) where load is constant

(b) where load changes frequently

(c) where constant operating speed is needed

(d) in none of the above situations.

44. For the same H.P. rating and full load speed, following motor has poor starting torque

(a) shunt

(b) series

(c) differentially compounded

(d) cumulativelyc’ompounded

45. In case of conductively compensated D.C. series motors, the compensating winding is provided

(a) as separately wound unit

(6) in parallel with armature winding

(c) in series with armature winding

(d) in parallel with field winding

46. Sparking at the commutator of a D.C. motor may result in

(a) damage to commutator segments

(b) damage to commutator insulation

(c) increased power consumption

(d) all of the above

47. Which of the following motor is preferred for operation in highly explosive atmosphere ?

(a) Series motor

(b) Shunt motor

(c) Air motor

(d) Battery operated motor

48. If the supply voltage for a D.C. motor is increased, which of the following will decrease ?

(a) Starting torque

(b) Operating speed

(c) Full-load current

(d) All of the above

49. Which one of the following is not the function of pole shoes in a D.C. machine ?

(a) To reduce eddy current loss

(b) To support the field coils

(c) To spread out flux for better uniformity

(d) To reduce the reluctance of the magnetic path

50. The mechanical power developed by a shunt motor will be maximum when the ratio of back e.m.f. to applied voltage is

(a) 4.0

(b) 2.0

(c) 1.0

(d) 0.5

51. The condition for maximum power in case of D.C. motor is

(a) back e.m.f. = 2 x supply voltage

(b) back e.m.f. = | x supply voltage

(c) supply voltage = | x back e.m.f.

(d) supply voltage = back e.m.f.

52. For which of the following applications a D.C. motor is preferred over an A.C. motor ?

(a) Low speed operation

(b) High speed operation

(c) Variable speed operation

(d) Fixed speed operation

53. In D.C. machines the residual magnetism is of the order of

(a) 2 to 3 per cent

(6) 10 to 15 per cent

(c) 20 to 25 per cent

(d) 50 to 75 per cent

54. Which D.C. motor is generally preferred for cranes and hoists ?

(a) Series motor

(b) Shunt motor

(c) Cumulatively compounded motor

(d) Differentially compounded motor

55. Three point starter can be used for

(a) series motor only

(b) shunt motor only

(c) compound motor only

(d) both shunt and compound motor

56. Sparking, is discouraged in a D.C. motor because

(a) it increases the input power con-sumption

(b) commutator gets damaged

(c) both (a) and (b)

(d) none of the above

57. Speed control by Ward Leonard method gives uniform speed variation

(a) in one direction

(b) in both directions

(c) below normal speed only

(d) above normal speed only.

58. Flywheel is used with D.C. compound motor to reduce the peak demand by the motor, compound motor will have to be

(a) level compounded

(b) under compounded

(c) cumulatively compounded

(d) differentially compounded

59. Following motor is used where high starting torque and wide speed range control is required.

(a) Single phase capacitor start

(b) Induction motor

(c) Synchronous motor

(d) D.C. motor

60. In a differentially compounded D.C. motor, if shunt field suddenly opens

(a) the motor will first stop and then run in opposite direction as series motor

(b) the motor will work as series motor and run at slow speed in the same direction

(c) the motor will work as series motor and run at high speed in the same direction

(d) the motor will not work and come to stop

61. Which of the following motor has the poorest speed regulation ?

(a) Shunt motor

(b) Series motor

(c) Differential compound motor

(d) Cumulative compound motor

62. Buses, trains, trolleys, hoists, cranes require high starting torque and therefore make use of

(a) D.C. series motor

(b) D.C. shunt motor

(c) induction motor

(d) all of above motors

63. As -the load is increased the speed of D.C. shunt motor will

(a) reduce slightly

(b) increase slightly

(c) increase proportionately

(d) remains unchanged

64. The armature torque of the D.C. shunt motor is proportional to

(a) field flux only

(b) armature current only

(c) both (a) and (b)

(d) none of the above

65. Which of the following method of speed control of D.C. machine will offer minimum efficiency ?

(a) Voltage control method

(b) Field control method

(c) Armature control method

(d) All above methods

1. Which of the following component is usually fabricated out of silicon steel ?

(a) Bearings

(b) Shaft

(c) Statorcore

(d) None of the above

2. The frame of an induction motor is usually made of

(a) silicon steel

(b) cast iron

(c) aluminium

(d) bronze

3. The shaft of an induction motor is made of

(a) stiff

(b) flexible

(c) hollow

(d) any of the above

4. The shaft of an induction motor is made of

(a) high speed steel

(b) stainless steel

(c) carbon steel

(d) cast iron

5. In an induction motor, no-load the slip is generally

(a) less than 1%

(b) 1.5%

(c) 2%

(d) 4%

6. In medium sized induction motors, the slip is generally around

(a) 0.04%

(b) 0.4%

(c) 4%

(d) 14%

7. In squirrel cage induction motors, the rotor slots are usually given slight skew

in order to

(a) reduce windage losses

(b) reduce eddy currents

(c) reduce accumulation of dirt and dust

(d) reduce magnetic hum

8. In case the air gap in an induction motor is increased

(a) the magnetising current of the rotor will decrease

(b) the power factor will decrease

(c) speed of motor will increase

(d) the windage losses will increase

9. Slip rings are usually made of

(a) copper

(b) carbon

(c) phospor bronze

(d) aluminium

10. A 3-phase 440 V, 50 Hz induction motor has 4% slip. The frequency of rotor

e.m.f. will be

(a) 200 Hz

(b) 50 Hz

(c) 2 Hz

(d) 0.2 Hz

11. In Ns is the synchronous speed and s the slip, then actual running speed of an

induction motor will be

(a) Ns

(b) s.N,

(c) (l-s)Ns

(d) (Ns-l)s

The efficiency of an induction motor can be expected to be nearly

(a) 60 to 90%

(b) 80 to 90%

(c) 95 to 98%

(d) 99%

13. The number of slip rings on a squirrel cage induction motor is usually

(a) two

(b) three
(c) four
(d) none
14. The starting torque of a squirrel-cage induction motor is
(a) low
(b) negligible
(c) same as full-load torque
(d) slightly more than full-load torque
15. A double squirrel-cage induction motor has
(a) two rotors moving in oppsite direction
(b) two parallel windings in stator
(c) two parallel windings in rotor
(d) two series windings in stator
16. Star-delta starting of motors is not possible in case of
(a) single phase motors
(b) variable speed motors
(c) low horse power motors
(d) high speed motors
17. The term 'cogging' is associated with
(a) three phase transformers
(b) compound generators
(c) D.C. series motors
(d) induction motors
18. In case of the induction motors the torque is
(a) inversely proportional to (Vslip)
(b) directly proportional to (slip)2
(c) inversely proportional to slip
(d) directly proportional to slip
19. An induction motor with 1000 r.p.m. speed will have
(a) 8 poles
(b) 6 poles
(c) 4 poles
(d) 2 poles
20. The good power factor of an induction motor can be achieved if the average
flux density in the air gap is
(a) absent
(b) small

(c) large
(d) infinity
21. An induction motor is identical to
(a) D.C. compound motor
(b) D.C. series motor
(c) synchronous motor
(d) asynchronous motor
22. The injected e.m.f. in the rotor of induction motor must have
(a) zero frequency
(b) the same frequency as the slip frequency
(c) the same phase as the rotor e.m.f.
(d) high value for the satisfactory speed control
23. Which of the following methods is easily applicable to control the speed of the
squirrel-cage induction motor ?
(a) By changing the number of stator poles
(b) Rotor rheostat control
(c) By operating two motors in cascade
(d) By injecting e.m.f. in the rotor circuit
24. The crawling in the induction motor is caused by
(a) low voltage supply
(b) high loads
(c) harmonics develped in the motor
(d) improper design of the machine
(e) none of the above
25. The auto-starters (using three auto transformers) can be used to start cage
induction motor of the following type
(a) star connected only
(b) delta connected only
(c) (a) and (b) both
(d) none of the above
26. The torque developed in the cage induction motor with autostarter is
(a) k/torque with direct switching
(6) K x torque with direct switching
(c) K2 x torque with direct switching
(d) k2/torque with direct switching

27. When the equivalent circuit diagram of doouble squirrel-cage induction motor

is constructed the two cages can be

considered

(a) in series

(b) in parallel

(c) in series-parallel

(d) in parallel with stator

28. It is advisable to avoid line-starting of induction motor and use starter

because

(a) motor takes five to seven times its full load current

(b) it will pick-up very high speed and may go out of step

(c) it will run in reverse direction

(d) starting torque is very high

29. Stepless speed control of induction motor is possible by which of the following methods ?

(a) e.m.f. injection in rotor eueuit

(b) Changing the number of poles

(c) Cascade operation

(d) None of the above

30. Rotor rheostat control method of speed control is used for

(a) squirrel-cage induction motors only

(b) slip ring induction motors only

(c) both (a) and (b)

(d) none of the above

31. In the circle diagram for induction motor, the diameter of the circle represents

(a) slip

(b) rotor current

(c) running torque

(d) line voltage

32. For which motor the speed can be controlled from rotor side ?

(a) Squirrel-cage induction motor

(b) Slip-ring induction motor

(c) Both (a) and (b)

(d) None of the above

33. If any two phases for an induction motor are interchanged

(a) the motor will run in reverse direction
(b) the motor will run at reduced speed
(c) the motor will not run
(d) the motor will burn

34. An induction motor is
(a) self-starting with zero torque
(b) self-starting with high torque
(c) self-starting with low torque
(d) non-self starting

35. The maximum torque in an induction motor depends on
(a) frequency
(b) rotor inductive reactance
(c) square of supply voltage
(d) all of the above

36. In three-phase squirrel-cage induction motors
(a) rotor conductor ends are short-circuited through slip rings
(b) rotor conductors are short-circuited through end rings
(c) rotor conductors are kept open
(d) rotor conductors are connected to insulation

37. In a three-phase induction motor, the number of poles in the rotor winding is always
(a) zero
(b) more than the number of poles in stator
(c) less than number of poles in stator
(d) equal to number of poles in stator

38. DOL starting of induction motors is usually restricted to
(a) low horsepower motors
(b) variable speed motors
(c) high horsepower motors
(d) high speed motors

39. The speed of a squirrel-cage induction motor can be controlled by all of the

following except
(a) changing supply frequency
(b) changing number of poles
(c) changing winding resistance
(d) reducing supply voltage

40. The 'crawling" in an induction motor is caused by

(a) high loads

(6) low voltage supply

(c) improper design of machine

(d) harmonics developed in the motor

41. The power factor of an induction motor under no-load conditions will be

closer to

(a) 0.2 lagging

(b) 0.2 leading

(c) 0.5 leading

(d) unity

42. The 'cogging' of an induction motor can be avoided by

(a) proper ventilation

(b) using DOL starter

(c) auto-transformer starter

(d) having number of rotor slots more or less than the number of stator slots (not equal)

43. If an induction motor with certain ratio of rotor to stator slots, runs at 1/7 of the normal speed, the phenomenon will be termed as

(a) humming

(b) hunting

(c) crawling

(d) cogging

44. Slip of an induction motor is negative when

(a) magnetic field and rotor rotate in opposite direction

(b) rotor speed is less than the synchronous speed of the field and are in the same direction

(c) rotor speed is more than the synchronous speed of the field and are in the same direction

(d) none of the above

45. Size of a high speed motor as compared to low speed motor for the same H.P. will be

(a) bigger

(b) smaller

(c) same

(d) any of the above

46. A 3-phase induction motor stator delta connected, is carrying full load and one of its fuses blows out. Then the motor

(a) will continue running burning its one phase

(b) will continue running burning its two phases

(c) will stop and carry heavy current causing permanent damage to its winding

(d) will continue running without any harm to the winding

47. A 3-phase induction motor delta connected is carrying too heavy load and oneof its fuses blows out. Then the motor

(a) will continue running burning its one phase

(b) will continue running burning its two phase

(c) will stop and carry heavy current causing permanent damage to its winding

(d) will continue running without any harm to the winding

48. Low voltage at motor terminals is due to

(a) inadequate motor wiring

(b) poorely regulated power supply

(c) any one of the above

(d) none of the above

49. In an induction motor the relationship between stator slots and rotor slots is that

(a) stator slots are equal to rotor slots

(b) stator slots are exact multiple of rotor slots

(c) stator slots are not exact multiple of rotor slots

(d) none of the above

50. Slip ring motor is recommended where

(a) speed control is required

(6) frequent starting, stopping and reversing is required

(c) high starting torque is needed

(d) all above features are required

51. As load on an induction motor goes on increasing

(a) its power factor goes on decreasing

(b) its power factor remains constant

(c) its power factor goes on increasing even after full load

(d) its power factor goes on increasing up to full load and then it falls again

52. If a 3-phase supply is given to the stator and rotor is short circuited rotor will move

(a) in the opposite direction as the direction of the rotating field

(b) in the same direction as the direction of the field

(c) in any direction depending upon phase squence of supply

53. It is advisable to avoid line starting of induction motor and use starter because

(a) it will run in reverse direction

(b) it will pick up very high speed and may go out of step

(c) motor takes five to seven times its full load current

(d) starting torque is very high

54. The speed characteristics of an induction motor closely resemble the speedload characteristics of which of the following machines

(a) D.C. series motor

(b) D.C. shunt motor

(c) universal motor

(d) none of the above

55. Which type of bearing is provided in small induction motors to support the rotor shaft ?

(a) Ball bearings

(b) Cast iron bearings

(c) Bush bearings

(d) None of the above

56. A pump induction motor is switched on to a supply 30% lower than its rated voltage. The pump runs. What will eventually happen ? It will

(a) stall after sometime

(b) stall immediately

(c) continue to run at lower speed without damage

(d) get heated and subsequently get damaged

57. 5 H.P., 50-Hz, 3-phase, 440 V, induction motors are available for the following r.p.m. Which motor will be the costliest ?

(a) 730 r.p.m.

(b) 960 r.p.m.

(c) 1440 r.p.m.

(d) 2880 r.p.m.

58. A 3-phase slip ring motor has

(a) double cage rotor

(b) wound rotor

(c) short-circuited rotor

(d) any of the above

59. The starting torque of a 3-phase squirrel cage induction motor is

(a) twice the full load torque

(b) 1.5 times the full load torque

(c) equal to full load torque

60. Short-circuit test on an induction motor cannot be used to determine

(a) windage losses

(b) copper losses

(c) transformation ratio

(d) power scale of circle diagram

61. In a three-phase induction motor

(a) iron losses in stator will be negligible as compared to that in rotor

(6) iron losses in motor will be neg¬ligible as compared to that in rotor

(c) iron losses in stator will be less than that in rotor

(d) iron losses in stator will be more than that in rotor

62. In case of 3-phase induction motors, plugging means

(a) pulling the motor directly on line without a starter

(b) locking of rotor due to harmonics

(c) starting the motor on load which is more than the rated load

(d) interchanging two supply phases for quick stopping

63. Which is of the following data is required to draw the circle diagram for an induction motor ?

(a) Block rotor test only

(b) No load test only

(c) Block rotor test and no-load test

(d) Block rotor test, no-load test and stator resistance test

64. In three-phase induction motors sometimes copper bars are placed deep in the rotor to

(a) improve starting torque

(b) reduce copper losses

(c) improve efficiency

(d) improve power factor

65. In a three-phase induction motor

(a) power factor at starting is high as compared to that while running

(b) power factor at starting is low as compared to that while running

(c) power factor at starting in the same as that while running

66. The vafcie of transformation ratio of an induction motor can be found by

(a) open-circuit test only

(b) short-circuit test only

(c) stator resistance test

(d) none of the above

67. The power scale of circle diagram of an induction motor can be found from

(a) stator resistance test

(b) no-load test only

(c) short-circuit test only

(d) noue of the above

68. The shape of the torque/slip curve of induction motor is

(a) parabola

(b) hyperbola

(c) rectangular parabola

(d) straigth line

69. A change of 4% of supply voltage to an induction motor will produce a change of appromimately

(a) 4% in the rotor torque

(b) 8% in the rotor torque

(c) 12% in the rotor torque

(d) 16% in the rotor torque

70. The stating torque of the slip ring induction motor can be increased by adding

(a) external inductance to the rotor

(b) external resistance to the rotor

(c) external capacitance to the rotor

(d) both resistance and inductance to rotor

71. A 500 kW, 3-phase, 440 volts, 50 Hz, A.C. induction motor has a speed of 960 r.p.m. on full load. The machine has 6 poles. The slip of the machine will be

(a) 0.01

(b) 0.02

(c) 0.03

(d) 0.04

72. The complete circle diagram of induetion motor can be drawn with the help of

data found from

(a) noload test

(6) blocked rotor test

(c) stator resistance test

(d) all of the above

73. In the squirrel-cage induction motor the rotor slots are usually given slight skew

(a) to reduce the magnetic hum and locking tendency of the rotor

(b) to increase the tensile strength of the rotor bars

(c) to ensure easy fabrication

(d) none of the above

74. The torque of a rotor in an induction motor under running condition is maximum

(a) at the unit value of slip

(b) at the zero value of slip

(c) at the value of the slip which makes rotor reactance per phase equal to the resistance per phase

(d) at the value of the slip which makes the rotor reactance half of the rotor

75. What will happen if the relative speed between the rotating flux of stator and rotor of the induction motor is zero ?

(a) The slip of the motor will be 5%

(b) The rotor will not run

(c) The rotor will run at very high speed

(d) The torque produced will be very large

76. The circle diagram for an induction motor cannot be used to determine

(a) efficiency

(b) power factor

(c) frequency

(d) output

77. Blocked rotor test on induction motors is used to find out

(a) leakage reactance

(b) power factor on short circuit

(c) short-circuit current under rated voltage

(d) all of the above

78. Lubricant used for ball bearing is usually

(a) graphite

(b) grease

(c) mineral oil

(d) molasses

79. An induction motor can run at synchronous speed when

(a) it is run on load

(b) it is run in reverse direction

(c) it is run on voltage higher than the rated voltage

(d) e.m.f. is injected in the rotor circuit

80. Which motor is preferred for use in mines where explosive gases exist ?

(a) Air motor

(b) Induction motor

(c) D.C. shunt motor

(d) Synchronous motor

81. The torque developed by a 3-phase induction motor least depends on

(a) rotor current

(b) rotor power factor

(c) rotor e.m.f.

(d) shaft diameter

82. In an induction motor if air-gap is increased

(a) the power factor will be low

(b) windage losses will be more

(c) bearing friction will reduce

(d) copper loss will reduce In an induction motor

83. In induction motor, percentage slip depends on

(a) supply frequency

(b) supply voltage

(c) copper losses in motor

(d) none of the above

85. In case of a double cage induction motor, the inner cage has

(a) high inductance arid low resistance

(b) low inductance and high resistance

(c) low inductance and low resistance

(d) high inductance and high resistance

86. The low power factor of induction motor is due to

(a) rotor leakage reactance

(b) stator reactance

(c) the reactive lagging magnetizing current necessary to generate the magnetic flux

(d) all of the above

87. Insertion of reactance in the rotor circuit

(a) reduces starting torque as well as maximum torque

(b) increases starting torque as well as maximum torque

(c) increases starting torque but maxi-mum torque remains unchanged

(d) increases starting torque but maxi-mum torque decreases

88. Insertion of resistance in the rotcir of an induction motor to develop a given torque

(a) decreases the rotor current

(b) increases the rotor current

(c) rotor current becomes zero

(d) rotor current rernains same

89. For driving high inertia loods best type of induction motor suggested is

(a) slip ring type

(b) squirrel cage type

(c) any of the above

(d) none of the above

90. Temperature of the stator winding of a three phase induction motor is

obtained by

(a) resistance rise method

(b) thermometer method

(c) embedded temperature method

(d) all above methods

91. The purpose of using short-circuit gear is

(a) to short circuit the rotor at slip rings

(b) to short circuit the starting resistances in the starter

(c) to short circuit the stator phase of motor to form star

(d) none of the above

92. In a squirrel cage motor the induced e.m.f. is

(a) dependent on the shaft loading

(b) dependent on the number of slots

(c) slip times the stand still e.m.f. induced in the rotor

(d) none of the above

93. Less maintenance troubles are experienced in case of

(a) slip ring induction motor

(b) squirrel cage induction motor

(c) both (a) and (b)

(d) none of the above

94. A squirrel cage induction motor is not selected when

(a) initial cost is the main consideration

(b) maintenance cost is to be kept low
(c) higher starting torque is the main consideration
(d) all above considerations are involved

95. Reduced voltage starter can be used with
(a) slip ring motor only but not with squirrel cage induction motor
(b) squirrel cage induction motor only but not with slip ring motor
(c) squirrel cage as well as slip ring induction motor
(d) none of the above

96. Slip ring motor is preferred over squirrel cage induction motor where
(a) high starting torque is required
(b) load torque is heavy
(c) heavy pull out torque is required
(d) all of the above

97. In a star-delta starter of an induction motor
(a) resistance is inserted in the stator
(b) reduced voltage is applied to the stator
(c) resistance is inserted in the rotor
(d) applied voltage perl stator phase is 57.7% of the line voltage

98. The torque of an induction motor is
(a) directly proportional to slip
(b) inversely proportional to slip
(c) proportional to the square of the slip
(d) none of the above

99. The rotor of an induction motor runs at
(a) synchronous speed
(b) below synchronous speed
(c) above synchronous speed
(d) any of the above

100. The starting torque of a three phase induction motor can be increased by
(a) increasing slip
(b) increasing current
(c) both (a) and (b)
(d) none of the above

1. Which of the following does not change in a transformer ?
(a) Current
(b) Voltage
(c) Frequency

(d) All of the above

2. In a transformer the energy is conveyed from primary to secondary

(a) through cooling coil

(b) through air

(c) by the flux

(d) none of the above

3. A transformer core is laminated to

(a) reduce hysteresis loss

(b) reduce eddy current losses

(c) reduce copper losses

(d) reduce all above losses

4. The degree of mechanical vibrations produced by the laminations of a transformer depends on

(a) tightness of clamping

(b) gauge of laminations

(c) size of laminations

(d) all of the above

5. The no-load current drawn by transformer is usually what per cent of the full load current ?

(a) 0.2 to 0.5 per cent

(b) 2 to 5 per cent

(c) 12 to 15 per cent

(d) 20 to 30 per cent

6. The path of a magnetic flux in a transformer should have

(a) high resistance

(b) high reluctance

(c) low resistance

(d) low reluctance

7. No-load on a transformer is carried out to determine

(a) copper loss

(b) magnetising current

(c) magnetising current and loss

(d) efficiency of the transformer

8. The dielectric strength of transformer oil is expected to be

(a) lkV

(b) 33 kV

(c) 100 kV

(d) 330 kV

9. Sumpner's test is conducted on trans-formers to determine

(a) temperature

(b) stray losses

(c) all-day efficiency

(d) none of the above

10. The permissible flux density in case of cold rolled grain oriented steel is around

(a) 1.7 Wb/m2

(b) 2.7 Wb/m2

(c) 3.7 Wb/m2

(d) 4.7 Wb/m2

11. The efficiency of a transformer will be maximum when

(a) copper losses = hysteresis losses

(b) hysteresis losses = eddy current losses

(c) eddy current losses = copper losses

(d) copper losses = iron losses

12. No-load current in a transformer

(a) lags behind the voltage by about 75°

(b) leads the voltage by about 75°

(c) lags behind the voltage by about 15°

(d) leads the voltage by about 15°

13. The purpose of providing an iron core in a transformer is to

(a) provide support to windings

(b) reduce hysteresis loss

(c) decrease the reluctance of the magnetic path

(d) reduce eddy current losses

14. Which of the following is not a part of transformer installation ?

(a) Conservator

(b) Breather

(c) Buchholz relay

(d) Exciter

15. While conducting short-circuit test on a transformer the following side is short circuited

(a) High voltage side

(b) Low voltage side

(c) Primary side

(d) Secondary side

16. In the transformer following winding has got more cross-sectional area

(a) Low voltage winding

(b) High voltage winding

(c) Primary winding

(d) Secondary winding

17. A transformer transforms

(a) voltage

(b) current

(c) power

(d) frequency

18. A transformer cannot raise or lower the voltage of a D.C. supply because

(a) there is no need to change the D.C. voltage

(b) a D.C. circuit has more losses

(c) Faraday's laws of electromagnetic induction are not valid since the rate of change of flux is zero

(d) none of the above

19. Primary winding of a transformer

(a) is always a low voltage winding

(b) is always a high voltage winding

(c) could either be a low voltage or high voltage winding

(d) none of the above

20. Which winding in a transformer has more number of turns ?

(a) Low voltage winding

(b) High voltage winding

(c) Primary winding

(d) Secondary winding

21. Efficiency of a power transformer is of the order of

(a) 100 per cent

(b) 98 per cent

(c) 50 per cent

(d) 25 per cent

22. In a given transformer for given applied voltage, losses which remain constant irrespective of load changes are

(a) friction and windage losses

(b) copper losses

(c) hysteresis and eddy current losses

(d) none of the above

23. A common method of cooling a power transformer is

(a) natural air cooling

(b) air blast cooling

(c) oil cooling

(d) any of the above

24. The no load current in a transformer lags behind the applied voltage by an angle of about

(a) 180°

(b) 120″

(c) 90°

(d) 75°

25. In a transformer routine efficiency depends upon

(a) supply frequency

(b) load current

(c) power factor of load

(d) both (b) and (c)

26. In the transformer the function of a conservator is to

(a) provide fresh air for cooling the transformer

(b) supply cooling oil to transformer in time of need

(c) protect the transformer from damage when oil expends due to heating

(d) none of the above

27. Natural oil cooling is used for transformers up to a rating of

(a) 3000 kVA

(b) 1000 kVA

(c) 500 kVA

(d) 250 kVA

28. Power transformers are designed to have maximum efficiency at

(a) nearly full load

(b) 70% full load

(c) 50% full load

(d) no load

29. The maximum efficiency of a distribution transformer is

(a) at no load

(b) at 50% full load

(c) at 80% full load

(d) at full load

30. Transformer breaths in when
(a) load on it increases
(b) load on it decreases
(c) load remains constant
(d) none of the above
31. No-load current of a transformer has
(a) has high magnitude and low power factor
(b) has high magnitude and high power factor
(c) has small magnitude and high power factor
(d) has small magnitude and low power factor
32. Spacers are provided between adjacent coils
(a) to provide free passage to the cooling oil
(b) to insulate the coils from each other
(c) both (a) and (b)
(d) none of the above
33. Greater the secondary leakage flux
(a) less will be the secondary induced e.m.f.
(b) less will be the primary induced e.m.f.
(c) less will be the primary terminal voltage
(d) none of the above
34. The purpose of providing iron core in a step-up transformer is
(a) to provide coupling between primary and secondary
(b) to increase the magnitude of mutual flux
(c) to decrease the magnitude of mag-netizing current
(d) to provide all above features
35. The power transformer is a constant
(a) voltage device
(b) current device
(c) power device
(d) main flux device
36. Two transformers operating in parallel will share the load depending upon their
(a) leakage reactance
(b) per unit impedance
(c) efficiencies
(d) ratings
37. If R2 is the resistance of secondary winding of the transformer and K is the transformation ratio then the equivalent secondary resistance

referred to primary will be

(a) R2/VK

(b) R2IK2

(c) R22!K2

(d) R22/K

38. What will happen if the transformers working in parallel are not connected with regard to polarity ?

(a) The power factor of the two trans-formers will be different from the power factor of common load

(b) Incorrect polarity will result in dead short circuit

(c) The transformers will not share load in proportion to their kVA ratings

(d) none of the above

39. If the percentage impedances of the two transformers working in parallel are different, then

(a) transformers will be overheated

(b) power factors of both the transformers will be same

(c) parallel operation will be not possible

(d) parallel operation will still be possible, but the power factors at which the two transformers operate will be different from the power factor of the common load

40. In a transformer the tappings are generally provided on

(a) primary side

(b) secondary side

(c) low voltage side

(d) high voltage side

41. The use of higher flux density in the transformer design

(a) reduces weight per kVA

(6) reduces iron losses

(c) reduces copper losses

(d) increases part load efficiency

42. The chemical used in breather for transformer should have the quality of

(a) ionizing air

(b) absorbing moisture

(c) cleansing the transformer oil

(d) cooling the transformer oil.

43. The chemical used in breather is

(a) asbestos fiber
(b) silica sand
(c) sodium chloride
(d) silica gel

45. The transformer ratings are usually expressed in terms of
(a) volts
(b) amperes
(c) kW
(d) kVA

46. The noise resulting from vibrations of laminations set by magnetic forces, is termed as
(a) magnetostrication
(b) boo
(c) hum
(d) zoom

47. Hysteresis loss in a transformer varies as CBmax = maximum flux density)
(a) Bmax
(b) Bmax1-6
(C) Bmax1-83
(d) B max

48. Material used for construction of transformer core is usually
(a) wood
(b) copper
(c) aluminium
(d) silicon steel

49. The thickness of laminations used in a transformer is usually
(a) 0.4 mm to 0.5 mm
(b) 4 mm to 5 mm
(c) 14 mm to 15 mm
(d) 25 mm to 40 mm

50. The function of conservator in a transformer is
(a) to project against'internal fault
(b) to reduce copper as well as core losses
(c) to cool the transformer oil
(d) to take care of the expansion and contraction of transformer oil due to variation of temperature of sur-roundings

51. The highest voltage for transmitting electrical power in India is

(a) 33 kV.
(6) 66 kV
(c) 132 kV
(d) 400 kV

52. In a transformer the resistance between its primary and secondary is
(a) zero
(b) 1 ohm
(c) 1000 ohms
(d) infinite

53. A transformer oil must be free from
(a) sludge
(b) odour
(c) gases
(d) moisture

54. A Buchholz relay can be installed on
(a) auto-transformers
(b) air-cooled transformers
(c) welding transformers
(d) oil cooled transformers

55. Gas is usually not liberated due to dissociation of transformer oil unless the oil temperature exceeds
(a) 50°C
(b) 80°C
(c) 100°C
(d) 150°C

56. The main reason for generation of harmonics in a transformer could be
(a) fluctuating load
(b) poor insulation
(c) mechanical vibrations
(d) saturation of core

57. Distribution transformers are generally designed for maximum efficiency around
(a) 90% load
(b) zero load
(c) 25% load
(d) 50% load

58. Which of the following property is not necessarily desirable in the material for transformer core ?

(a) Mechanical strength

(6) Low hysteresis loss

(c) High thermal conductivity

(d) High permeability

59. Star/star transformers work satisfactorily when

(a) load is unbalanced only

(b) load is balanced only

(c) on balanced as well as unbalanced loads

(d) none of the above

60. Delta/star transformer works satisfactorily when

(a) load is balanced only

(b) load is unbalanced only

(c) on balanced as well as unbalanced loads

(d) none of the above

61. Buchholz's relay gives warning and protection against

(a) electrical fault inside the transformer itself

(b) electrical fault outside the transformer in outgoing feeder

(c) for both outside and inside faults

(d) none of the above

62. The magnetising current of a transformer is usually small because it has

(a) small air gap

(b) large leakage flux

(c) laminated silicon steel core

(d) fewer rotating parts

63. Which of the following does not change in an ordinary transformer ?

(a) Frequency

(b) Voltage

(c) Current

(d) Any of the above

64. Which of the following properties is not necessarily desirable for the material for transformer core ?

(a) Low hysteresis loss

(b) High permeability

(c) High thermal conductivity

(d) Adequate mechanical strength

65. The leakage flux in a transformer depends upon
(a) load current
(b) load current and voltage
(c) load current, voltage and frequency
(d) load current, voltage, frequency and power factor
66. The path of the magnetic flux in transformer should have
(a) high reluctance
(b) low reactance
(c) high resistance
(d) low resistance
67. Noise level test in a transformer is a
(a) special test
(b) routine test
(c) type test
(d) none of the above
68. Which of the following is not a routine test on transformers ?
(a) Core insulation voltage test
(b) Impedance test
(c) Radio interference test
(d) Polarity test
69. A transformer can have zero voltage regulation at
(a) leading power factor
(b) lagging power factor
(c) unity power factor
(d) zero power factor
70. Helical coils can be used on
(a) low voltage side of high kVA transformers
(b) high frequency transformers
(c) high voltage side of small capacity transformers
(d) high voltage side of high kVA rating transformers
1. The commercial sources of energy are
(a) solar, wind and biomass
(b) fossil fuels, hydropower and nuclear energy
(c) wood, animal wastes and agriculture wastes
(d) none of the above
3. In India largest thermal power station is located at
(a) Kota
(b) Sarni

(c) Chandrapur
(d) Neyveli
4. The percentage O2 by Weight in atmospheric air is
(a) 18%
(b) 23%
(c) 77%
(d) 79%
5. The percentage 02 by volume in atmosphere air is
(a) 21%
(b) 23%
(c) 77%
(d) 79%
6. The proper indication of incomplete combustion is
(a) high CO content in flue gases at exit
(b) high CO2 content in flue gases at exit
(c) high temperature of flue gases
(d) the smoking exhaust from chimney
7. The main source of production of biogas is
(a) human waste
(b) wet cow dung
(c) wet livestock waste
(d) all above
8. India's first nuclear power plant was installed at
(a) Tarapore
(b) Kota
(c) Kalpakkam
(d) none of the above
9. In fuel cell, the _______ energy is converted into electrical energy.
(a) mechanical
(b) chemical
(c) heat
(d) sound
10. Solar thermal power generation can be achieved by
(a) using focusing collector or heliostates
(b) using flat plate collectors
(c) using a solar pond
(d) any of the above system
51. In case of impulse steam turbine

(a) there is enthalpy drop in fixed and moving blades

(b) there is enthalpy drop only in moving blades

(c) there is enthalpy drop in nozzles

(d) none of the above

52. The pressure on the two sides of the impulse wheel of a steam turbine

(a) is same

(b) is different

(c) increases from one side to the other side

(d) decreases from one side to the other side

53. In De Laval steam turbine

(a) the pressure in the turbine rotor is approximately same as in con¬denser

(b) the pressure in the turbine rotor is higher than pressure in the con¬denser

(c) the pressure in the turbine rotor gradually decreases from inlet to exit from

condenser

(d) none from the above

54. Incase of reaction steam turbine

(a) there is enthalpy drop both in fixed and moving blades

(b) there is enthalpy drop only in fixed blades

(c) there is enthalpy drop only in moving blades

(d) none of the above

55. Curtis turbine is

(a) reaction steam turbine

(b) pressure velocity compounded steam turbine

(c) pressure compounded impulse steam turbine

(d) velocity compounded impulse steam turbine

56. Rateau steam turbine is

(a) reaction steam turbine

(b) velocity compounded impulse steam turbine

(c) pressure compounded impulse steam turbine

(d) pressure velocity compounded steam turbine

57. Parson's turbine is

(a) pressure compounded steam turbine

(b) simple single wheel, impulse steam turbine

(c) simple single wheel reaction steam turbine

(d) multi wheel reaction steam turbine

58. For Parson's reaction steam turbine, degree of reaction is

(a) 75%

(b) 100%

(c) 50%

(d) 60%

59. Reheat factor in steam turbines depends on

(a) exit pressure only

(b) stage efficiency only

(c) initial pressures and temperature only

(d) all of the above

60. The value of reheat factor normally varies from

(a) 0.5 to 0.6

(b) 0.9 to 0.95

(c) 1.02 to 1.06

(d) 1.2 to 1.6

61. Steam turbines are governed by the following methods

(a) Throttle governing

(b) Nozzle control governing

(c) By-pass governing

(d) all of the above

62. In steam turbines the reheat factor

(a) increases with the increase in number of stages

(b) decreases with the increase in number of stages

(c) remains same irrespective of number of stages

(d) none of the above

63. The thermal efficiency of the engine with condenser as compared to without

condenser, for a given pressure and temperature of steam, is

(a) higher

(b) lower

(c) same as long as initial pressure and temperature is unchanged

(d) none of the above

64. In jet type condensers

(a) cooling water passes through tubes and steam surrounds them

(b) steam passes through tubes and cooling water surrounds them

(c) steam and cooling water mix

(d) steam and cooling water do not mix

65. In a shell and tube surface condenser

(a) steam and cooling water mix to give the condensate

(b) cooling water passes through the tubes and steam surrounds them

(c) steam passes through the cooling tubes and cooling water surrounds them

(d) all of the above varying with situation

66. In a surface condenser if air is removed, there is

(a) fall in absolute pressure maintained in condenser

(b) rise in absolute pressure maintained in condenser

(c) no change in absolute pressure in the condenser

(d) rise in temperature of condensed steam

67. The cooling section in the surface condenser

(a) increases the quantity of vapour extracted along with air

(b) reduces the quantity of vapour extracted along with air

(c) does not affect vapour quantity extracted but reduces pump capacity of air

extraction pump

(d) none of the above

68. Edward's air pump

(a) removes air and also vapour from condenser

(b) removes only air from condenser

(c) removes only un-condensed vapour from condenser

(d) removes air alongwith vapour and also the condensed water from condenser

69. In a steam power plant, the function of a condenser is

(a) to maintain pressure below atmospheric to increase work output from the

primemover

(b) to receive large volumes of steam exhausted from steam prime mover

(c) to condense large volumes of steam to water which may be used again in boiler

(d) all of the above

70. In a regenerative surface condenser

(a) there is one pump to remove air and condensate

(b) there are two pumps to remove air and condensate

(c) there are three pumps to remove air, vapour and condensate

(d) there is no pump, the condensate gets removed by gravity

71. Evaporative type of condenser has

(a) steam in pipes surrounded by water
(b) water in pipes surrounded by steam
(c) either (a) or (b)
(d) none of the above

72. Pipes carrying steam are generally made up of
(a) steel
(b) cast iron
(c) copper
(d) aluminium

73. For the safety of a steam boiler the number of safety valves fitted are
(a) four
(b) three
(c) two
(d) one

74. Steam turbines commonly used in steam power station are
(a) condensing type
(b) non-condensing type
(c) none of the above

75. Belt conveyer can be used to transport coal at inclinations upto
(a) 30°
(b) 60°
(c) 80°
(d) 90°

76. The maximum length of a screw conveyer is about
(a) 30 metres
(b) 40 metres
(c) 60 metres
(d) 100 metres

77. The efficiency of a modern boiler using coal and heat recovery equipment is
about
(a) 25 to 30%
(b) 40 to 50%
(c) 65 to 70%
(d) 85 to 90%

78. The average ash content in Indian coals is about
(a) 5%
(b) 10%

(c) 15%

(d) 20%

79. Load center in a power station is

(a) center of coal fields

(b) center of maximum load of equipments

(c) center of gravity of electrical system

80. Steam pressure in a steam power station, which is usually kept now-a-days is

of the order of

(a) 20 kgf/cm2

(b) 50 kgf/cm2

(c) 100 kgf/cm2

(d) 150 kgf/cm2

81. Economisers improve boiler efficiency by

(a) 1 to 5%

(b) 4 to 10%

(c) 10 to 12%

82. The capacity of large turbo-generators varies from

(a) 20 to 100 MW

(b) 50 to 300 MW

(c) 70 to 400 MW

(d) 100 to 650 MW

83. Caking coals are those which

(a) burn completely

(b) burn freely

(c) do not form ash

(d) form lumps or masses of coke

84. Primary air is that air which is used to

(a) reduce the flame length

(b) increase the flame length

(c) transport and dry the coal

(d) provide air around burners for get¬ting optimum combustion

85. Secondary air is the air used to

(a) reduce the flame length

(b) increase the flame length

(c) transport and dry the coal

(d) provide air round the burners for getting optimum combustion

86. In coal preparation plant, magnetic separators are used to remove

(a) dust
(b) clinkers
(c) iron particles
(d) sand

88. Method which is commonly applied for unloading the coal for small power
plant is
(a) lift trucks
(b) coal accelerators
(c) tower cranes
(d) belt conveyor

89. Bucket elevators are used for
(a) carrying coal in horizontal direction
(b) carrying coal in vertical direction
(c) carrying coal in any direction

90. The amount of air which is supplied for complete combustion is called
(a) primary air
(b) secondary air
(c) tertiary air

91. In ______ system fuel from a central pulverizing unit is delivered to a bunker
and then to the various burners
(a) unit
(b) central
(c) none of the above

92. Under-feed stokers work best for ______ coals high in volatile matter and
with caking tendency
(a) anthracite
(b) lignite
(c) semibituminous and bituminous

93. Example of overfeed type stoker is
(a) chain grate
(b) spreader
(c) travelling grate
(d) all of the above

94. Where unpulverised coal has to be used and boiler capacity is large, the stoker

which is used is

(a) underfeed stoker

(b) overfeed stoker

(c) any

96. Blowing down of boiler water is the process

(a) to reduce the boiler pressure

(b) to increase the steam temperature

(c) to control the solid concentration in the boiler water by removing some of the

concentrated saline water

(d) none of the above

97. Deaerative heating is done to

(a) heat the water

(b) heat the air in the water

(c) remove dissolved gases in the water

98. Reheat factor is the ratio of

(a) isentropic heat drop to useful heat drop

(b) adiabatic heat drop to isentropic heat drop

(c) cumulative actual enthalpy drop for the stages to total is isentropic enthalpy

heat drop

100. Compounding of steam turbine is done for

(a) reducing the work done

(b) increasing the rotor speed

(c) reducing the rotor speed

(d) balancing the turbine

1. By which of the following systems electric power may be transmitted ?

(a) Overhead system

(b) Underground system

(c) Both (a) and (b)

(d) None of the above

2 are the conductors, which connect the consumer's terminals to the distribution

(a) Distributors

(b) Service mains

(c) Feeders
(d) None of the above

3. The underground system cannot be operated above
(a) 440 V
(b) 11 kV
(c) 33 kV
(d) 66 kV

4. Overhead system can be designed for operation up to
(a) 11 kV
(b) 33 kV
(c) 66 kV
(d) 400 kV

5. If variable part of annual cost on account of interest and depreciation on the capital outlay is equal to the annual cost of electrical energy wasted in the conductors, the total annual cost will be minimum and the corresponding size of conductor will be most economical. This statement is known as
(a) Kelvin's law
(b) Ohm's law
(c) Kirchhoffs law
(d) Faraday's law

6. The wooden poles well impregnated with creosite oil or any preservative compound have life
(a) from 2 to 5 years
(b) 10 to 15 years
(c) 25 to 30 years
(d) 60 to 70 years

7. Which of the following materials is not used for transmission and distribution of electrical power ?
(a) Copper
(b) Aluminium
(c) Steel
(d) Tungsten

8. Galvanised steel wire is generally used as
(a) stay wire
(b) earth wire
(c) structural components
(d) all of the above

9. The usual spans with R.C.C. poles are
(a) 40—50 meters
(b) 60—100 meters
(c) 80—100 meters
(d) 300—500 meters

10. The corona is considerably affected by which of the following ?
(a) Size of the conductor
(b) Shape of the conductor
(c) Surface condition of the conductor
(d) All of the above

11. Which of the following are the constants of the transmission lines ?
(a) Resistance
(b) Inductance
(c) Capacitance
(d) All of the above

12. 310 km line is considered as
(a) a long line
(b) a medium line
(c) a short line
(d) any of the above

13. The phenomenon qf rise in voltage at the receiving end of the open-circuited or lightly loaded line is called the
(a) Seeback effect
(b) Ferranti effect
(c) Raman effect
(d) none of the above

14. The square root of the ratio of line impedance and shunt admittance is called the
(a) surge impedance of the line
(b) conductance of the line
(c) regulation of the line
(d) none of the above

15. Which of the following is the demerit of a 'constant voltage transmission system' ?
(a) Increase of short-circuit current of the system
(b) Availability of steady voltage at all loads at the line terminals

(c) Possibility of better protection for the line due to possible use of higher terminal reactants

(d) Improvement of power factor at times of moderate and heavy loads

(e) Possibility of carrying increased power for a given conductor size in case of long-distance heavy power transmission

17. The operating voltage of high voltage cables is up to

(a)l.lkV

(b)3.3kV

(c)6.6kV

(d)llkV

18. The operating voltage of supertension cables is up to

(a) 3.3 kV

(b) 6.6 kV

(c) 11 kV

(d) 33 kV

19. The operating voltage of extra high tension cables is upto

(a) 6.6 kV

(b) 11 kV

(c) 33 kV

(d) 66 kV

20. Which of the following methods is used for laying of underground cables ?

(a) Direct laying

(b) Draw-in-system

(c) Solid system

(d) All of the above

22. Due to which of the following reasons the cables should not be operated too hot ?

(a) The oil may loose its viscosity and it may start drawing off from higher levels

(b) Expansion of the oil may cause the sheath to burst

(c) Unequal expansion may create voids in the insulation which will lead to ionization

(d) All of the above

23. Which of the following D.C. distribution system is the simplest and lowest in first cost ?

(a) Radial system

(b) Ring system

(c) Inter-connected system
(d) None of the above
24. A booster is a
(a) series wound generator
(b) shunt wound generator
(c) synchronous generator
(d) none of the above
25. Besides a method of trial and error, which of the following methods is employed for solution of network problems in interconnected system ?
(a) Circulating current method
(b) Thevenin's theorem
(c) Superposition of currents
(d) All of the above
28. The voltage of the single phase supply to residential consumers is
(a) 110 V
(b) 210 V
(c) 230 V
(d) 400 V
29. Most of the high voltage transmission lines in India are
(a) underground
(b) overhead
(c) either of the above
(d) none of the above
30. The distributors for residential areas are
(a) single phase
(b) three-phase three wire
(c) three-phase four wire
(d) none of the above
32. High voltage transmission lines use
(a) suspension insulators
(b) pin insulators
(c) both (a) and (b)
(d) none of the above
33. Multicore cables generally use
(a) square conductors
(b) circular conductors
(c) rectangular conductors
(d) sector-shaped conductors

34. Distribution lines in India generally use
(a) wooden poles
(b) R.C.C. poles
(c) steel towers
(d) none of the above
35. The material commonly used for insulation in high voltage cables is
(a) lead
(b) paper
(c) rubber
(d) none of the above
36. The loads on distributors systems are generally
(a) balanced
(b) unbalanced
(c) either of the above
(d) none of the above
37. The power factor of industrial loads is generally
(a) unity
(b) lagging
(c) leading
(d) zero
38. Overhead lines generally use
(a) copper conductors
(b) all aluminium conductors
(c) A.C.S.R. conductors
(d) none of these
39. In transmission lines the cross-arms are made of
(a) copper
(b) wood
(c) R.C.C.
(d) steel
40. The material generally used for armour of high voltage cables is
(a) aluminium
(b) steel
(c) brass
(d) copper
42. The material commonly used for sheaths of underground cables is
(a) lead
(b) rubber

(c) copper

(d) iron

43. The minimum clearance between the ground and a 220 kV line is about

(a) 4.3 m

(b) 5.5 m

(c) 7.0 m

(d) 10.5 m

44. The spacing between phase conductors of a 220 kV line is approximately equal to

(a) 2 m

(b) 3.5 m

(c) 6 m

(d) 8.5 m

45. Large industrial consumers are supplied electrical energy at

(a) 400 V

(b) 11 kV

(c) 66 kV

(d) 400 kV

48. Transmitted power remaining the same, if supply voltage of a D.C. 2-wire

feeder is increased 100 percent, saving in copper is

(a) 25 percent

(b) 50 percent

(c) 75 percent

(d) 100 percent

49. A uniformly-loaded D.C. distributor is fed at both ends with equal voltages. As compared to a similar distributor fed at one end only, the drop at the middle point is

(a) one-fourth

(b) one-third

(c) one-half

(d) twice

50. As compared to a 2-wire D.C. distributor, a 3-wire distributor with same maximum voltage to earth uses only

(a) 31.25 percent of copper

(b) 33.3 percent of copper

(c) 66.7 percent of copper

(d) 125 percent of copper

51. Which of the following is usually not the generating voltage ?

(a) 6.6 kV

(b) 8.8 kV

(c) 11 kV

(d) 13.2 kV

52. For an overhead line, the surge impedance is taken as

(a) 20-30 ohms

(b) 70—80 ohms

(c) 100—200 ohms

(d) 500—1000 ohms

Ans: c

53. The presence of ozone due to corona is harmful because it

(a) reduces power factor

(b) corrodes the material

(c) gives odour

(d) transfer energy to the ground

54. A feeder, in a transmission system, feeds power to

(a) distributors

(b) generating stations

(c) service mains

(d) all of the above

55. The power transmitted will be maximum when

(a) corona losses are minimum

(b) reactance is high

(c) sending end voltage is more

(d) receiving end voltage is more

56. A 3-phase 4 wire system is commonly used on

(a) primary transmission

(b) secondary transmission

(c) primary distribution

(d) secondary distribution

57. Which of the following materials is used for overhead transmission lines ?

(a) Steel cored aluminium

(b) Galvanised steel

(c) Cadmium copper

(d) Any of the above

58. Which of the following is not a constituent for making porcelain insulators ?

(a) Quartz
(b) Kaolin
(c) Felspar
(d) Silica

59. There is a greater possibility of occurence of corona during

(a) dry weather
(b) winter
(c) summer heat
(d) humid weather

60. Which of the following relays is used on long transmission lines ?

(a) Impedance relay
(b) Mho's relay
(c) Reactance relay
(d) None of the above

61. The steel used in steel cored conductors is usually

(a) alloy steel
(b) stainless steel
(c) mild steel
(d) high speed steel

62. Which of the following distribution systems is more reliable ?

(a) Radial system
(b) Tree system
(c) Ring main system
(d) All are equally reliable

63. Which of the following characteristics should the line supports for transmission lines possess ?

(a) Low cost
(b) High mechanical strength
(c) Longer life
(d) All of the above

64. Transmission voltage of ll kV is normally used for distances upto

(a) 20—25 km
(b) 40—50 km
(c) 60—70 km
(d) 80—100 km

65. Which of the following regulations is considered best?

(a) 50%

(b) 20%

(c) 10%

(d) 2%

66. Skin effect is proportional to

(a) (conductor diameter)

(b) (conductor diameter)

(c) (conductor diameter)

(d) (conductor diameter)

67. A conductor, due to sag between two supports, takes the form of

(a) semi-circle

(b) triangle

(c) ellipse

(d) catenary

68. In AC.S.R. conductors, the insulation between aluminium and steel conductors is

(a) insulin

(b) bitumen

(c) varnish

(d) no insulation is required

69. Which of the following bus-bar schemes has the lowest cost ?

(a) Ring bus-bar scheme

(b) Single bus-bar scheme

(c) Breaker and a half scheme

(d) Main and transfer scheme

71. By which of the following methods string efficiency can be improved ?

(a) Using a guard ring

(b) Grading the insulator

(c) Using long cross arm

(d) Any of the above

72. In aluminium conductors, steel core is provided to

(a) compensate for skin effect

(b) neutralise proximity effect

(c) reduce line inductance

(d) increase the tensile strength

73. By which of the following a bus-bar is rated ?

(a) Current only

(b) Current and voltage

(c) Current, voltage and frequency

(d) Current, voltage, frequency and short time current

74. A circuit is disconnected by isolators when

(a) line is energized

(b) there is no current in the line

(c) line is on full load

(d) circuit breaker is not open

75. For which of the following equipment current rating is not necessary ?

(a) Circuit breakers

(b) Isolators

(c) Load break switch

(d) Circuit breakers and load break switches

76. In a substation the following equipment is not installed

(a) exciters

(b) series capacitors

(c) shunt reactors

(d) voltatre transformers

77. jCorona usually occurs when the electrostatic stress in air around the conductor exceeds

(a) 6.6 kV (r.m.s. value)/cm

(b) 11 kV (r.m.s. value)/cm

(c) 22 kV (maximum value)/cm

(d) 30 kV (maximum value)/cm

78. The voltage drop, for constant voltage transmission is compensated by installing

(a) inductors

(b) capacitors

(c) synchronous motors

(d) all of above

(e) none of the above

79. The use of strain type insulators is made where the conductors are

(a) dead ended

(b) at intermediate anchor towers

(c) any of the above

(d) none of the above

80. The current drawn by the line due to corona losses is

(a) non-sinusoidal
(b) sinusoidal
(c) triangular
(d) square

81. Pin type insulators are generally not used for voltages beyond
(a) 1 kV
(b) 11 kV
(c) 22 kV
(d) 33 kV

82. Aluminium has a specific gravity of
(a) 1.5
(b) 2.7
(c) 4.2
(d) 7.8

83. For transmission of power over a distance of 200 km, the transmission voltage should be
(a) 132 kV
(b) 66 kV
(c) 33 kV
(d) 11 kV

84. For aluminium, as compared to copper, all the following factors have higher values except
(a) specific volume
(b) electrical conductivity
(c) co-efficient of linear expansion
(d) resistance per unit length for same cross-section

85. Which of the following equipment, for regulating the voltage in distribution feeder, will be most economical ?
(a) Static condenser
(b) Synchronous condenser
(c) Tap changing transformer
(d) Booster transformer

86. In a tap changing transformer, the tappings are provided on
(a) primary winding
(b) secondary winding
(c) high voltage winding
(d) any of the above

87. Constant voltage transmission entails the following disadvantage

(a) large conductor area is required for same power transmission

(b) short-circuit current of the system is increased

(c) either of the above

(d) none of the above

88. On which of the following factors skin effect depends ?

(a) Frequency of the current

(b) Size of the conductor

(c) Resistivity of the conductor material

(d) All of the above

89. The effect of corona can be detected by

(a) presence of ozone detected by odour

(b) hissing sound

(c) faint luminous glow of bluish colour

(d) all of the above

90. For transmission of power over a distance of 500 km, the transmission voltage should be in the range

(a) 150 to 220 kV

(b) 100 to 120 kV

(c) 60 to 100 kV

(d) 20 to 50 kV

91. In the analysis of which of the following lines shunt capacitance is neglected ?

(a) Short transmission lines

(b) Medium transmission lines

(c) Long transmission lines

(d) Medium as well as long transmission lines

92. When the interconnector between two stations has large reactance

(a) the transfer of power will take place with voltage fluctuation and noise

(b) the transfer of power will take place with least loss

(c) the stations will fall out of step be¬cause of large angular displacement between the stations

(d) none of the above

93. The frequency of voltage generated, in case of generators, can be increased by

(a) using reactors

(b) increasing the load

(c) adjusting the governor

(d) reducing the terminal voltage

(e) none of the above

94. When an alternator connected to the bus-bar is shut down the bus-bar voltage will

(a) fall

(b) rise

(c) remain unchanged

(d) none of the above

95. The angular displacement between two interconnected stations is mainly due to

(a) armature reactance of both alternators

(b) reactance of the interconnector

(c) synchronous reactance of both the alternators

(d) all of the above

96. Electro-mechanical voltage regulators are generally used in

(a) reactors

(b) generators

(c) transformers

(d) all of the above

97. Series capacitors on transmission lines are of little use when the load VAR requirement is

(a) large

(b) small

(c) fluctuating

(d) any of the above

98. The voltage regulation in magnetic amplifier type voltage regulator is effected by

(a) electromagnetic induction

(b) varying the resistance

(c) varying the reactance

(d) variable transformer

99. When a conductor carries more current on the surface as compared to core, it is due to

(a) permeability variation

(b) corona

(c) skin effect

(d) unsymmetrical fault

(e) none of the above

100. The following system is not generally used

(a) 1-phase 3 wire

(b) 1-phase 4 wire

(c) 3-phase 3 wire

(d) 3-phase 4 wire

www.ingramcontent.com/pod-product-compliance
Ingram Content Group UK Ltd.
Pitfield, Milton Keynes, MK11 3LW, UK
UKHW021920190726
13853UKWH00002B/761